Leveraging Resources
for *Student Success*

Leveraging Resources for *Student Success*

How School Leaders Build Equity

Mary Ann Burke • Reynaldo Baca
Lawrence O. Picus • Cathy E. Jones

CORWIN PRESS, INC.
A Sage Publications Company
Thousand Oaks, California

For information:

Corwin Press, Inc.
A Sage Publications Company
2455 Teller Road
Thousand Oaks, California 91320
www.corwinpress.com

Sage Publications Ltd.
6 Bonhill Street
London EC2A 4PU
United Kingdom

Sage Publications India Pvt. Ltd.
M-32 Market
Greater Kailash I
New Delhi 110 048 India

Printed in the United States of America

Library of Congress Cataloging-in-Publication Data

Leveraging resources for student success: How school leaders build
equity / Mary Ann Burke . . . [et al.].
    p. cm.
Includes bibliographical references and index.
  ISBN 0-7619-4545-8 (c: acid-free paper) — ISBN 0-7619-4546-6
(p: acid-free paper)
  1. Urban schools—United States—Administration. 2. Community and
school—United States. 3. Children with social
disabilities—Education—United States. 4. Academic achievement—United
States. 5. Educational equalization—United States. I. Burke, Mary Ann.
  LC5131 .L436 2003
  379.2'6—dc21   20020051800

This book is printed on acid-free paper.

03 04 05 06 10 9 8 7 6 5 4 3 2 1

Acquisitions Editor:	Robb Clouse
Editorial Assistant:	Erin Clow
Copy Editor:	Jon Preimesberger
Typesetter:	C&M Digitals (P) Ltd
Proofreader:	Scott Oney
Production Editor:	Diane S. Foster
Indexer:	Will Ragsdale
Cover Designer:	Tracy E. Miller
Production Designer:	Michelle Lee

Contents

Preface

As more states require districtwide standardized testing for student promotion and graduation, principals and teachers are struggling with how to best serve their underserved student populations. Educational reform strategies include parent education, community involvement, academic support services, school reorganizations, and curricular changes. Current reform strategies provide principals and teacher leaders with limited training in how to adapt educational services for multicultural and economically diverse student populations. The equitable access of educational services is becoming a critical reform theme as school principals and teacher leaders struggle in how to involve underserved families in their students' academic preparation. The struggle continues as principals and teachers try to identify the best methods that will remediate what students must learn to pass standardized examinations.

Cathy Jones, an urban school practitioner for more than thirty years, and Mary Ann Burke, a community planner, grantwriter, and district office grants administrator, partnered with Reynaldo Baca, an educational sociologist and bilingual education program developer, and Lawrence O. Picus, an educational economist, to create this book, which the authors feel represents the best culturally proficient strategies in responding to the multicultural needs of urban school families. When working with diverse community groups, Jones and Burke have observed that principals and teacher leaders have not been effective in differentiating resources for these groups. Burke created the strategies described in this book for mobilizing communities into planning programs for culturally and economically diverse students.

ORGANIZATION OF THIS BOOK ■

This book examines strategies that can help culturally and economically diverse students access resources, services, and an appropriate education. As schools become more culturally diverse, it is critical for principals and teachers to create policies and procedures that ensure effective interactions among students and their teachers. A school staff's systematic focus on diversity enhances the educational opportunities of all students (Lindsey, Robins, & Terrell, 1999). By merging multicultural staff development training with the resource access strategies used by effective principals, this book's intent is to create a new level of understanding for all principals and teacher leaders in how to best help students reach their highest academic and career development potential.

Chapter 1 describes effective principal and teacher leadership strategies that have been used in urban schools to help economically challenged and racially diverse student populations access services.

Chapter 2 describes social justice practices, values, beliefs, and goals in urban schools that can increase access to educational services for economically challenged and culturally diverse student populations.

Chapter 3 includes practices of schools and communities working together as equal partners to eliminate the racial and economic disparities among all students. Individual differences of various cultural communities can be created by forming effective community relations campaigns, problem-solving coalitions, and resource development partnerships.

Chapter 4 describes how principals and teacher leaders can equitably leverage and distribute resources among diverse student populations. The chapter emphasizes strategies for building powerful community coalitions, shortcuts for writing program grants, and methods of collaboration with diverse organizations.

Chapter 5 describes how program evaluation instruments must adequately evaluate economically challenged and culturally diverse students. The chapter includes sample evaluation templates that can authentically measure changes in students' academic performance.

Chapter 6 summarizes multiple strategies that principals and teacher leaders can use for responding to the diverse needs of culturally and economically diverse students. The chapter provides examples of how a culturally proficient and community supported school can enhance the academic and career development needs of all of its students.

■ ACKNOWLEDGMENTS

This book represents over 30 years of field research in urban schools and communities. It challenges what is currently being taught to teachers and principals in their teacher preparation and administrative credentialing university programs. By merging the expertise of school principals and teacher leaders with field-based research, this book provides readers with specific strategies that will increase their productivity and survival skills in serving culturally diverse and economically challenged communities of students. Our work represents the contributions of many urban practitioners and researchers. We thank Lee Mahon and Mitsu Kumagai, who have served as mentors for more than a decade in developing effective community coalitions for accessing academic resources for diverse community groups. Stuart Gothold from the Rossier School of Education at the University of Southern California has provided transformational leadership in challenging our beliefs of traditional leadership strategies for urban schools. William B. Michael from the Division of Educational Psychology and Technology in the Rossier School of Education at the University of Southern California has helped us create alternative assessment instruments that effectively measure the impact of remedial and enrichment programs on diverse students' academic achievement. Jacques Bordeaux has provided us with a vision of how urban students and their families can partner with teachers and businesses to prepare students for acceptance into competitive higher educational institutions, and for careers in science and math.

Special thanks go to Yvette King-Berg from Project GRAD Los Angeles; Karen Matsui, from the Achievement Council; and Cambria Smith from the Volunteer Center of Los Angeles, who have provided us with countless hours of guidance on how to create innovative programs that equalize service delivery systems for underachieving youth.

Appreciation goes to Magaly Lavadenz from Loyola Marymount University, Rossier School of Education former Dean Guilbert C. Hentschke, and Rossier School of Education former professional studies manager Jeffrey Davis for sponsoring and coordinating the continuing education program components.

We would not have been able to complete the ongoing research for this project without the commitment and sponsorship from Compton Unified School District. Special thanks to former State Administrator Dr. Randolph Ward and Compliance Administrator Tom Brown, who have challenged our thinking in how to design academic programs and manage schools that will ensure academic success for all students.

Finally, our love and thanks go to our families and friends, who have provided us with the time and the emotional nourishment required to undertake the challenges of overcoming academic isolation and access to educational services for all our students.

The contributions of the following reviewers are gratefully acknowledged:

Jeffery Maiden
Associate Professor
Educational Administration, Curriculum and Supervision
University of Oklahoma
Norman, OK

James J. Ritchie
Dean
School of Education and Human Resources
University of Bridgeport
Bridgeport, CT

Robert Derlin
Associate Director
Institutional Research, Planning, & Outcomes Assessment
New Mexico State University
Las Cruces, NM

John Spiesman
Educational Consultant
Ohio

Scott McLeod
Assistant Professor
College of Education and Human Development
University of Minnesota
Minneapolis, MN

CORWIN PRESS

The Corwin Press logo—a raven striding across an open book—represents the happy union of courage and learning. We are a professional-level publisher of books and journals for K-12 educators, and we are committed to creating and providing resources that embody these qualities. Corwin's motto is "Success for All Learners."

About the Authors

 **Mary Ann Burke** is an Adjunct Lecturer in school finance, grantwriting and systematic planning, and school-community relations at the California State University, Sacramento. She is also an Adjunct Assistant Professor in the Rossier School of Education at the University of Southern California specializing in resource development for education. She has provided administrative program development, grantwriting assistance, and assessment support to various Los Angeles County urban school districts and charter schools. Burke is the former Director of the Community Partnership Coalition VISTA Project sponsored by Fenton Avenue Charter School. The project recruits and trains parent and community volunteers to serve as mentors and tutors in the classroom. She is the author of *Simplified Grantwriting* and coauthor of *Recruiting Volunteers*, *Creative Fundraising*, and *Developing Community-Empowered Schools*.

 **Reynaldo Baca** is Research Professor of Education and Codirector of the Center for Multilingual Multicultural Research in the Rossier School of Education at the University of Southern California. In this capacity, he oversees the direction of the Latino and Language Minority Teacher Project designed for paraeducators becoming bilingual teachers, the Bank of America–funded Beginning Support and Assessment Induction Program for K–3 Teachers of Language Minority Students, and the CMMR Doctoral Fellowship Program in Language Minority Teacher Education. He serves on the editorial board of *Teacher Education Quarterly*, as Program Director for the Sociology of Education Association, as consultant on teacher education to the U.S. Department of Education, and as program evaluator for school reform at several school districts across the nation. He has recently completed a five-year middle school access project involving the scaffolding of the gifted and talented curriculum for high potential language minority students. His research interests and publications focus on the social organization of immigration in Los Angeles, the sociology of education, and explanatory models for minority student achievement.

 **Lawrence O. Picus** is Professor and Chair of the Division of Policy and Administration in the Rossier School of Education at the University of Southern California. He also serves as the Director of the Center for Research in Education Finance (CREF), a school finance research center housed at the Rossier School of Education. CREF research focuses on issues of school finance and productivity. His current research interests focus on adequacy and equity in school finance as well as efficiency and productivity in the provision of educational programs for K-12 schoolchildren. Recent work has also included analyses of fiscal implications of vouchers and charter schools.

Picus is past President of the American Education Finance Association. He is author of *In Search of Productive Schools*, and coauthor of *School Finance: A Policy Perspective*, and *Principles of School Business Administration*. In addition, he is the Senior Editor of the 1995 yearbook of the American Education Finance Association, *Where Does the Money Go? Resource Allocation in Elementary and Secondary Schools*. He has published numerous articles in professional journals as well. He is a former member of the Editorial Advisory Committee of the Association of School Business Officials, International, and he has served as a consultant to the National Education Association, American Federation of Teachers, the National Center for Education Statistics, WestEd, and to the states of Washington, Vermont, Oregon, Wyoming, South Carolina, Louisiana, and Arkansas.

 **Cathy Jones** is a Director at California State University, Dominguez Hills, in the Teacher Education Department for the Alternative Credential Internship Program and the Director of the Beginning Teacher Support Assessment (BTSA) Program. The BTSA Program serves a four-district consortium. Jones was a 35-year employee of the Long Beach Unified School District and a former consultant with the Compton Unified School District (CUSD), where she worked as the Accountability Officer facilitating a $5 million desegregation grant that employed a staff of 153. She also served as a staff development trainer and coordinated the district's strategic planning process, implemented procedures, and provided program evaluation. Jones has a long history of service in public education, starting in 1968 as an elementary school teacher in Kansas City, MO. She earned the bachelor's in education at Emporia State Teacher's College and a master's in urban education administration from Pepperdine University.

1

Principal and Teacher Leadership Strategies

The leadership of the principal and teachers in an urban, economically challenged, and culturally diverse school community requires effective perseverance. These school leaders must continually respond to the community's needs of creating a safe and equitable school environment for all its student groups. A significant number of the day-to-day operational decisions in challenged schools are made by the school's principal and teacher leaders. Their responsiveness and data-driven decision making can affect the school site's access to equitable educational services.

The sections of this chapter describe effective principal and teacher leadership survival strategies that have been used in urban schools. These nine practices are the following:

1. Defining your school's culture

2. Leading with vision, conviction, and honesty

3. Prioritizing relationships instead of efficiency

4. Defining district protocol at the beginning of any process

5. Using effective strategic planning and time management strategies

6. Being flexible and adaptable to do whatever it takes to achieve results within the policies and procedures of the school district

7. Recruiting the best people for the job and establishing career paths for retention

8. Determining how principals and teachers wear many hats

9. Creating checkpoints for accountability

These survival strategies can ensure that students will receive equitable access to the district's educational services regardless of the family's income, home language, prior experience with the American school system, and prior formalized school experiences. All the practices that are described in this chapter must consider a school's culture; the leadership style of principals and teacher leaders; the protocol process and flexibility for program development; recruitment strategies; and accountability strategies.

■ SURVIVAL STRATEGY #1: DEFINING A SCHOOL'S CULTURE

A school's culture includes the traditions, beliefs, policies, and norms within a school that can be shaped, enhanced, and maintained through a school's leaders (Short & Greer, 1997). Typical questions that can be asked of a school community about its culture include the following:

- How do various community groups describe their role within the school?
- How does the school respond to the individual learning needs of students?
- How does the school assess the academic achievement of various groups of students?
- How do the school's principal and teachers get along with students and their families?
- How do the principal and the teachers get along?
- How does the school relate to its community groups?

A school's culture can best be changed by (a) making visible changes in its structure and processes; (b) modifying its philosophies, goals, and strategies; and (c) bringing about a change in the assumptions of various school and community groups (Short & Greer, 1997). When a school's culture supports the assumption that all students have the capacity to learn and achieve, the staff and students have the freedom to modify previously held philosophies about how students learn. With the belief that all students can achieve, a school's principal and teachers can explore alternative strategies to help underachieving students become successful. Within this philosophical framework, a school's principal and teachers can develop literacy programs that serve the unique learning needs of second language learners, students from economically challenged families, and students who have special education needs. The most effective school principals and teachers typically develop a holistic support network of supplementary student services for underachieving students. Effective intervention services for diverse learners include the following:

- Basic skill curriculum taught through the arts
- Basic skill tutorial support services offered during the school day
- Short-term remedial class instruction offered during the school day
- Mentoring support activities in the community that reinforce basic skills
- Community-based service learning activities that are structured to reinforce basic skills
- Saturday academic enrichment programs to support students and their families
- Family literacy programs that address the unique cultural needs of a community

Schools that encourage community groups to develop supplementary student programs should provide the following support services (Burke & Picus, 2001):

- An orderly and well-maintained school facility that assures community members that the students are valued
- An approachable staff who can refer non–English speakers to appropriate bilingual staff for assistance
- Policies and procedures that are clearly articulated and available for review
- School newsletters and communication materials describing various school activities
- A process for working with community groups in providing supplemental student services
- A comprehensive volunteer development program for community members to support students in the classroom and through supplemental programs
- A school-based donation and fundraising program for community members to make donations of supplies, equipment, and contributions for various activities

Figure 1.1 provides a worksheet for a school's principal and teachers to identify effective strategies that they currently use and strategies that they can develop to improve the overall cultural practices in their school.

SURVIVAL STRATEGY #2: LEADING WITH VISION, CONVICTION, AND HONESTY

An effective principal or teacher leader must lead with vision, trust his or her convictions, and honestly communicate a code of ethics. The principal's or teacher leader's vision and integrity must be based on realistic facts, predictions, and trends (Bennis & Goldsmith, 1997). A principal's or teacher leader's encompassing vision for student achievement should include the contributions of various community groups. When students, parents, community members, and staff request access to academic services, the principal and teacher leaders must consider the fairness of data-driven decision making. Reinforcing the consequences of various decisions requires courage, perseverance, and creativity. When decisions are clearly understood, various community groups can accept and respect the consequences of the leader's decisions.

Figure 1.1. School Culture Worksheet

In the left column, list effective strategies that your principal and teachers currently use that contribute to a healthy school culture and belief that all students can achieve academically. In the right column list strategies that your principal and teachers can develop to improve the overall culture in your school.

Description of the Current School's Culture	Description of How to Change the School's Culture
Organizational structure and processes:	Organizational structure and processes:
Philosophies:	Philosophies:
Goals and strategies:	Goals and strategies:
Assumptions:	Assumptions:
Short-term prioritized action plan:	Proposed short-term prioritized action plan:
Long-term prioritized action plan:	Proposed long-term prioritized action plan:

Effective principals and teacher leaders can only control what they have been given responsibility for and what they can do personally about a situation. A principal's or teacher leader's success can best be defined by the perceived favorable impact of the leader's actions by various community groups. When a principal or teacher leader gains a clearer understanding of his or her school's culture and community, the principal or teacher leader can modify existing school practices and beliefs to better meet the needs of diverse student groups.

School leaders can lead with vision, conviction, and honesty when they are able to accomplish the following:

- Clearly articulate how a program should be developed
- Convince the other teachers and community members about the value of the change
- Empower students and various stakeholder groups to develop new programs that support the vision
- Support the vision and be willing to assist all stakeholders in developing new programs that reinforce the vision
- Admit that new program development may be difficult and that there may need to be changes as obstacles are identified
- Acknowledge the limitations of newly developed programs and be prepared to make changes to ensure success
- Take responsibility for any mistakes during the development of new programs
- Share all successes with stakeholder groups
- Confer with the students and the various stakeholder groups to verify what is working and not working in a new program
- Have the courage to walk away from failures and be prepared to create another new program
- Continuously evaluate whether specific programs meet the unique learning needs of diverse student groups

Figure 1.2 provides a worksheet for a school's principal and teacher leaders to (a) identify the demographic profile of their school community; (b) define the demographic characteristics and needs of specific school groups; (c) develop a school's vision that will support the academic success of diverse student populations; and (d) consider an academic plan of action for various underachieving student groups.

SURVIVAL STRATEGY #3: PRIORITIZING RELATIONSHIPS INSTEAD OF EFFICIENCY

Effective principals and teacher leaders build a safety net of supporters they can trust. They are also prepared to approach a wide range of individuals for advice and support when situations become challenging. The current trend to focus on the efficiency of school operations and on the accountability of student performance has limited the amount of time school principals and teacher leaders have to effectively nurture students (Short & Greer, 1997). In response to this challenge, effective school principals and teacher leaders create changes that empower the school's staff through participative

Figure 1.2. Defining Your Vision for Responding to Your School's Needs

Step #1: In the table below, complete demographic profile information about your school.

Characteristic	Description of the Characteristic
Geographical location and community description	
Ethnic composition of the student population	
Income makeup of the students	
Data describing student needs (i.e., percentage of students who are limited-English-proficient or qualify for free lunch or special education services)	
Types of programs and intervention services provided	
Experience and training of the school's teachers and staff	
Types of partnerships with community organizations	
Other	

Figure 1.2. Defining Your Vision for Responding to Your School's Needs

Step #2: Using information compiled in Step #1, define the overall characteristics and needs for specific student populations in your school in the table below.

Identified Student Group	Characteristics and Needs for Specific Group
Low-income students	
Students from multistressed home environments	
Students from specific ethnic communities	
Limited-English-Proficient students	
Students with special needs	
Students at risk of failing	
Other	
Other	

Figure 1.2. Defining Your Vision for Responding to Your School's Needs

Step #3: Using the information compiled about your school in the tables above, construct a vision that will support the academic success of all your students.

Our Vision for Student Success:

Step #4: Create a plan for action in responding to this vision for your identified community groups in the table below.

Type of Stakeholder	Plan for Action
Students	
Teachers	
Staff	
Parents	
Community	
Business	
Government	
Media	
Other	

decision making. Participative decision making encourages principals, teacher leaders, students, and the school community to collectively build effective relationships that can contribute to the development of educational programs that foster student achievement.

When a school's principal and teacher leaders focus on building relationships with diverse stakeholders for program development, the school's leaders can effectively implement program changes that are responsive to all of their students. Effective relationship skill development includes the following strategies (Bennis & Goldsmith, 1997):

- Training teachers and community groups to use empathy when working with students and the school leaders in designing new programs
- Providing supportive feedback about how the various stakeholders are supporting students in their achievement
- Seeking reactions and eliciting suggested changes from various stakeholders to ensure that all stakeholders' concerns about a program design are being considered for best results
- Listening attentively to any criticism and acknowledging the value of input from the various stakeholder groups

Figure 1.3 provides a worksheet for principals and teacher leaders to identify strategies that can help build effective partnerships and relationship skills with various stakeholder groups to support student achievement.

Review the information that you have compiled in Figure 1.3. Consider other types of decision making and academic support activities that you can have each stakeholder group participate in at your school site in Figure 1.4. You may want to convene a brainstorming session with your various stakeholder groups to complete the proposed academic support activity chart. This activity can be part of a strategic planning process on meeting the unique learning needs of your diverse student community.

SURVIVAL STRATEGY #4: DEFINING DISTRICT PROTOCOL AT THE BEGINNING OF ANY PROCESS

Before initiating any changes in a new process, it is important for school leaders to confirm what the district protocol has been for a specific activity. By identifying and defining the school district's traditional protocol process, school leaders can eliminate obstacles while implementing changes. Many urban school districts have formalized procedures established for implementing new programs, practices, and initiatives. When a school can clearly articulate to its stakeholders what the district's protocol process is for a specific activity, the stakeholders will have a clear understanding of various problem-solving options. A school's stakeholders can also determine which teacher leaders can provide added support.

Figure 1.3. School Relationship Building Worksheet

In the chart below, (a) list each stakeholder group in your school,
(b) identify specific decision-making activities for each stakeholder group,
and (c) identify specific activities each group participates in that can impact
student achievement.

Stakeholder Group	Decision-Making Activities	Academic Support Activities
School leaders		
Teachers		
Support staff		
Students		
Parents		
Community agencies		
Community members		
Businesses		
Other		

At times, a school district's protocol's process may be different from other schools in the district. For example, when a school wants to create a new program that will be staffed by a community agency, the school leader should follow the district's policies and procedures to hire a subcontractor. Listed below are examples of policies and procedures that should be considered when hiring a subcontractor for a new program:

1. Review the district's policies and procedures for creating a new program.

2. Determine what specific policies pertain to hiring a subcontractor.

3. Identify the specific conditions for hiring a particular subcontractor without having to obtain multiple bids.

4. Determine what paperwork must be completed and how many bids must be received for larger contracts.

5. Identify the timeline and activities that are required before hiring a subcontractor.

6. Determine how the subcontractor should be monitored.

Figure 1.4. Proposed Academic Support Activity Chart

Stakeholder Group	Proposed Decision-Making Activities	Proposed Academic Support Activities
School leaders		
Teachers		
Support staff		
Students		
Parents		
Community agencies		
Community members		
Businesses		
Other		

7. Have the subcontractor prepare a timeline of specific activities and deliverables.

8. Define how and when the subcontractor will be paid for services.

9. Determine what insurance liability policies the subcontractor must submit after the bid is accepted.

10. Define how to terminate a contract for unsatisfactory performance.

11. Consider how to expand a contract for additional services.

12. Identify specific departments and key contacts that must be communicated with during the development of the bid and completion of a contract.

If the school's principal or teacher leader has followed the appropriate district-defined process, the school leader can track specific paperwork if a problem is encountered. Once a problem occurs, the school leader should follow the district's protocol process. The protocol process may require that the school's principal or teacher leader must contact a specific district-level staff member for resolution. The timeline for contacting specific individuals may be critical for resolving the problem. If a school's principal or teacher leader does not understand the district's informal process for problem resolution, he or she may have great difficulty resolving a problem.

Understanding a school district's protocol process may be critical for effectively implementing a change. Whenever a school's principal or teacher leader intends to initiate a change, the school principal or teacher leader should consider the following strategies:

1. Study and understand the impact of change on various stakeholders.

2. Contact other schools within the district and in the community that have successfully implemented the same type of change to discuss effective implementation and protocol strategies.

3. Request and study the school district's policies and procedures for initiating and implementing a specific change.

4. Contact key district leaders to discuss effective strategies and protocol procedures that can support the change process.

5. Identify who should be contacted in specific departments when challenges occur.

6. Enlist the support of key district staff to resolve all problems in a timely manner.

7. Remain positive throughout the change process to strengthen relationships with key contacts and stakeholder groups.

Figure 1.5 provides a worksheet for school principals and teacher leaders to identify various school district policies and protocol procedures that can support changes in a school's philosophy, goals, strategies, or processes.

■ SURVIVAL STRATEGY #5: USING EFFECTIVE STRATEGIC PLANNING AND TIME MANAGEMENT STRATEGIES

Using effective strategic planning and time management strategies can have a direct impact on a program's development. When principals and teacher leaders consider how strategic planning and time management can be incorporated in any change process, the results can encourage the school's stakeholders in supporting further changes. Poorly managed program development can deter making changes in the future. Effective strategic planning and time management strategies include the following:

1. Plan for the strategic planning process and collect pertinent data about the school and its community.

2. Determine which stakeholders should be involved in the planning process.

3. Identify specific outcomes that the school's leadership intends to achieve through the process.

4. Create a strategic planning process agenda with a listing of specific activities.

5. Compile information about the school's mission statement, its demographic composition, and a brief description of current programs that the school provides.

Figure 1.5. Identifying School District Policies and Protocol Procedures
Worksheet

1. Describe the program, goal, strategy, or philosophy that the school intends to change:
2. List individuals in the district and community who have implemented the change:
3. Summarize the district's policies and procedures that support the change:
4. List district contacts who can identify protocol procedures to support the change:
5. List department contacts who can support problem resolution:
6. List key district staff who can support problem resolution in a timely manner:
7. List staff members who can keep you positively focused in the change process:

6. Disseminate all information and the agenda one week before the event. This will provide participants with sufficient time to prepare for the meeting.

7. At the strategic planning session, review the school's mission, its cultural values and beliefs, its demographic profile, and its program offerings with all session participants.

8. Share all community data with the session participants.

9. Once all school and community information has been shared with the participants, review the goals and objectives for the day, and brainstorm solutions to the school community's needs.

10. Brainstorm solutions as one large group or break into smaller groups to address specific needs.

11. Each problem solution should include its benefits and limitations. Once smaller groups have brainstormed various solutions, all participants should review and cluster the solutions into subgroups representing larger solutions for various needs. The major solutions can then be prioritized to determine which solutions will best respond to the immediate needs of the school's students.

12. Once solutions are prioritized, the group can identify existing community services that can respond to various needs.

13. The group can also identify any gaps in service delivery.

14. Service delivery gaps can eventually be addressed by creating grant proposals for program development and funding.

15. The strategic planning process should conclude by summarizing the action steps with a timeline, and by designating individuals who will integrate and implement the various action items.

16. The strategic planning process should also include an action plan for evaluating the various implementation activities quarterly to determine how effectively the plan is being implemented and to make adjustments as required.

Figure 1.6 provides a strategic planning worksheet for school leaders to use for creating a strategic planning session with an ongoing evaluation follow-up plan.

■ SURVIVAL STRATEGY #6: BEING FLEXIBLE AND ADAPTABLE TO DO WHATEVER IT TAKES TO ACHIEVE RESULTS WITHIN THE POLICIES AND PROCEDURES OF THE SCHOOL DISTRICT

Once a school's stakeholders have determined how they will create and implement new programs and processes within the school, it is vital for all of the stakeholders to be flexible and adaptable during the implementation process. Many principals and teacher leaders must resort to heroic measures to achieve results within a specific time frame in a multistressed school and district environment. For example, a school's principal may be required to check the paperwork that has been submitted to the district office to hire a subcontractor on a daily basis. In many urban and multistressed school communities, the contract submission and signoff process can become delayed because the central office staff is busy responding to the demanding survival needs of its student community. Although it should not be the principal's job to track contracts, a few encouraging words to an overextended central office staff will probably expedite the process.

When principals and teacher leaders are forced to become more actively involved in the daily operations of a school district, these leaders should consider the following strategies:

1. Identify specific activities that must occur at the school site and at the district office to support the school site's daily operations and new program development

2. Check on an appropriate timeline for each activity

3. Identify specific offices and key contacts for completing all activities

4. Contact key contacts and define an appropriate timeline for completing each activity

Figure 1.6. School Site Strategic Planning Worksheet

Step 1: List the types of data that will be collected to support the planning process. School site data can include the ethnic composition of students, income levels of families, number of English language proficient, test score data, school services, etc. Community data can include ethnic composition, health and human care statistics, employment date, crime rates, literacy rates, and education achievement levels.

Step 2: List the stakeholders who should be involved in the process.

Step 3: List the outcomes that you want to achieve in this process.

(Continued)

Figure 1.6. Continued

Step 4: List the specific agenda activities and timeline for the planning session that will support the anticipated outcomes.
Step 5: List the information that will be included with the agenda including the school's mission statement, its demographic data, and current programs. Disseminate this information to all participants one week before the planning session.
Step 6: Create an action plan form that will include the action plan steps with a timeline, and the designated individuals for implementing various steps.
Step 7: Create an action plan for quarterly evaluation of various implementation activities.

5. Brainstorm how the principal and teacher leaders at the school site will support each other in the various activities

6. Create a plan of action on how the principal and teacher leaders at the school site will adjust and modify their schedules if problems should occur at the district office

7. Develop a plan of action on how the school will overcome obstacles

8. Identify how the school has previously overcome obstacles satisfactorily

9. Determine how each school leader can ensure that a new program will overcome previous obstacles

10. Identify other school staff who can support a program's implementation and the daily challenges at the school site

11. Maintain ongoing dialogue among school leaders to coordinate problem resolution efforts at the district office

12. Build healthy relationships with district office staff, subcontractors, and other school stakeholders to ensure that future challenges can be addressed with minimal disruption

Figure 1.7 provides a reflective worksheet for principals and teacher leaders to use in brainstorming a follow-up plan for new program development. The more prepared a principal or teacher leader is in predicting obstacles, the less frustrated and stressed all stakeholders will be in the program implementation process.

SURVIVAL STRATEGY #7: RECRUITING THE BEST PEOPLE FOR THE JOB AND ESTABLISHING CAREER PATHS FOR RETENTION

Recruiting and developing the most qualified staff to work with a culturally and economically diverse student population can ensure a program's success. Effective recruitment strategies include the following (Burke & Liljenstolpe, 1992; Burke & Picus, 2001):

- Recruit and cross-train existing staff for new responsibilities and job promotions
- Recruit prospective employees initially as part-time contractors to evaluate their effectiveness in responding to the needs of a new project
- Recruit new employees through educational internship programs from colleges and universities
- Network through colleagues to identify prospective employees
- Identify prospective employees through services provided by other contractors
- Recruit new employees through school-based volunteers and mentors
- Recruit employees through company-sponsored community service projects

Figure 1.7. School Site Problem Resolution Worksheet for Program
Implementation

❑ Considering the policies and procedures of your school district to institute this new program or process, describe the process you intend to use for full implementation.
❑ What specific obstacles or challenges have you consistently experienced in implementing similar changes at your school site?
❑ How have you satisfactorily solved obstacles and challenges in the past?
❑ Who in the district office or at other school sites has provided you with significant support in resolving program implementation problems?
❑ What can you do in your role to ensure that the implementation process will overcome previous obstacles and challenges that you have experienced?
❑ What can other staff at your school site do to support you in this implementation process?

- Solicit referrals through trade, rehabilitation, and job training programs

Once a principal or teacher leader has hired the appropriate staff to support a new program, the school leader should provide ongoing training opportunities. Staff development training should build all employees' skills. The training should focus on how staff members can integrate and support other programs and functions within the school (Burke & Liljenstolpe, 1992). Effective staff development training should be designed to accomplish the following goals (Hutson, 1981; Joyce & Showers, 1980):

- Use adult learning theories and provide opportunities for practice
- Provide immediate feedback on performance-related tasks
- Focus on job-related responsibilities with adequate resources
- Emphasize motivation, skill acquisition, and career-long growth
- Include collaborative planning, goal setting, activity development, and feedback
- Combine theory, modeling, practice, feedback, and coaching in training activities
- Design a long-term staff development process with an emphasis on intrinsic professional rewards.

Figure 1.8 provides a worksheet for principals and teacher leaders to list the various types of staff development training strategies that can support their school's teachers and staff in developing new programs. The worksheet can help school leaders identify the specific types of training strategies and activities that can meet the unique learning needs of their staff.

SURVIVAL STRATEGY #8: DETERMINING HOW PRINCIPALS AND TEACHER LEADERS WEAR MANY HATS

When working in multistressed schools and districts, principals and teacher leaders must wear many hats to be able to initiate change and fully implement a new program and process. Typically, a principal or teacher leader must lead his or her staff in supporting all school site activities related to a new program. Support activities can include the following:

- Creating and leading a strategic planning process for identifying what changes must occur at the school site to better meet the unique learning needs of the school's students
- Drafting and tracking the completion of the paperwork, contracts, and any grant submission requirements for new project development
- Representing the school's needs and program development at key school district and community meetings
- Providing the inspirational support and technical assistance to staff in program development

Figure 1.8. Job and Career Path Staff Development Training

Staff Development Topic	Type of Training Activities and Methods
Job induction training	Theory, modeling, practice, feedback, and coaching in training activities
Communication skill development and training	Adult learning theory strategies and practice with immediate feedback
Child development	Theory, modeling, practice, and feedback
Project management and resource development training	Business management skill development using modeling and adult learning theories
Curriculum content and development for students	Theory, modeling, practice, feedback, and coaching in training activities
Specific type of training:	
Specify type of training:	
Specify type of training:	
Specify type of training:	

- Helping the staff design an effective training program for successful program or process implementation
- Doing whatever it may take within the policies and procedures of the school district to follow through and advocate for school site change

Principals and school leaders must learn how to adjust to the various roles required to develop new projects when the district office staff and the support staff become overwhelmed with their daily responsibilities. Effective strategies for juggling multiple roles include the following:

1. Clarify the specific activities that must be pursued to fully implement a new program

2. Determine the specific skills that will be required to support other roles in the implementation process

3. Consider the skills required for the program development team and determine who can best support the various roles required for developing the new program

4. Identify alternate staff members at the school site or at the district office that can provide support in identified areas of weakness

5. Continuously support the program development team's growth in areas of weakness

6. Provide ongoing staff development training in computer literacy, contract negotiations, conflict management, communication, leadership, finance, and accounting to increase the school staff's skill development

7. Identify other community groups and individuals that can assist in the program's development

Figure 1.9 provides a reflective worksheet that the school principal and teacher leaders can use to identify their specific roles in a new program. Use the form to identify the other roles required for follow-through on developing an innovative program.

SURVIVAL STRATEGY #9: CREATING CHECKPOINTS FOR ACCOUNTABILITY ■

During the initial stages of implementing a new program, principals and teacher leaders must develop a process for checking the activities that have been completed within a specific time interval by a designated and responsible staff member. Checkpoints for accountability can include the following strategies:

1. Identify the various activities required to fully implement a new program at the school site

2. Create an action plan with timeline and designated staff members to complete each activity

3. Review the action plan each week and determine what specific activities must be completed

4. Follow up with designated staff members listed in the action plan

5. Determine if specific program activities are being completed according to the proposed schedule

6. Meet weekly with all program staff to determine how effectively the program is being implemented

7. Facilitate quarterly strategic planning sessions to evaluate a program's outcomes

Figure 1.9. Identify the Many Roles of the Principal and Teacher Leaders to Support a Program's Development

Check or List the Current Roles You Serve at Your School Site	Check or List the Roles You Must Serve to Support New Program Development
Principal/teacher leader	
Strategic planner	
Curriculum developer	
Staff development trainer	
Resource developer	
Parent educator	
Counselor	
Other:	
Other:	

8. Create a schedule of what program data must be collected to measure program outcomes

9. Collect the data required for measuring results and outcomes

10. Facilitate quarterly focus groups with program participants to clarify the validity of the outcomes and the data being collected

11. Construct and circulate program surveys and questionnaires to various stakeholders on the content and quality of the program or process development

12. Evaluate the data and feedback that has been collected to identify key themes

Figure 1.10 on page 24 provides a sample checkpoint accountability plan for a School Day Tutorial Program for Underachieving Students. An accountability plan can assist principals and teacher leaders in providing the necessary support required for fully implementing a new school-based program. The sample checkpoint accountability plan in Figure 1.10 illustrates how a school's staff can design a program development tracking instrument.

The nine leadership survival strategies described in this chapter will not guarantee that all students will receive an equitable education. These survival practices can provide principals and school leaders with basic tools for developing an academic environment that can benefit all students. Chapter 2 considers social justice strategies that principals and teachers can use when working with culturally and economically diverse urban students. Chapters 3 through 6 provide principals and other school leaders with strategies on how to build community partnerships for the effective use of limited resources for diverse student populations.

Figure 1.10.   Sample Checkpoint Accountability Plan for a School Day Tutorial Program for Underachieving Students

Project Activity	Designated Staff	Timeline	Accountability Instruments
Hire five teachers to provide individual and small group tutorial support for a total of 60 underachieving students each day.	Principal	7/1/XX– 9/1/XX	A total of five teachers will be processed for employment with teaching contracts by 9/1/XX.
Train five teachers in tutorial strategies that support the school's adopted reading program.	Reading Specialist	9/1/XX– 10/1/XX	All five teachers will demonstrate appropriate tutorial strategies using the school's adopted reading program.
Identify 60 students who are currently reading below grade level according to the diagnostic reading tests given to all students during the first two weeks of the school year.	Reading Specialist	9/1/XX– 9/15/XX	The 60 students selected for the program will demonstrate below grade level reading abilities as demonstrated in their diagnostic test results.
75% of the 60 students who were reading below grade level will show gains in their reading abilities as documented in the reading diagnostic testing given to all students participating in the program at the end of six weeks.	Reading Specialist	9/15/XX– 10/30/XX	75% of the 60 students selected for the program will demonstrate increases in their reading abilities as demonstrated in their diagnostic test results.
60% of the 60 students who have participated in the daily tutorial program since 9/15/XX will be reading at grade level by the end of the first semester as documented in the diagnostic reading test administered at the end of the semester.	Reading Specialist	9/15/XX– 1/30/XX	60% of the 60 students selected for the program will demonstrate that they are reading at grade level as demonstrated in their diagnostic test results.

2

Social Justice for Diverse Students

Although many urban students continue to attend segregated schools, the struggle for inclusive and socially just practices has persevered. Since the mid-1950s, educational initiatives, court cases, and federal funding have focused on school desegregation, compensatory education, Head Start early childhood education programs, educational remedies for language minority students, and programs for physically challenged students. The 1983 *Nation at Risk* report by the National Commission on Excellence and Equity and the 1994 passage of the Goals 2000: Educate America Act) emphasized the need for schools to develop new programs to support culturally and economically diverse students in their academic achievement (Jennings, 1995).

Since the 1990s, cultural proficiency or a belief that all children and youth can learn well in their own neighborhoods and can have access to an equal distribution of resources in urban schools has prevailed (Lindsey, Robins, & Terrell, 1999). Research shows that desegregation can result in better opportunity networks for minority students without any loss for white students (Orfield, Eaton, and the Harvard Project on School Desegregation, 1996). More recent research has demonstrated how working-class ethnic minority youth can create social webs to ensure school success (Stanton-Salazar, 2001).

How urban, multistressed, and underperforming schools meet the need of educating students in their neighborhoods continues to challenge policymakers and educators as new funding initiatives are enacted to meet their needs. Some of the most progressive programs have become reform models and are being replicated nationally in a variety of communities. To date, many of these promising practices appear to be helping students make some academic gains, but no one program appears to be surfacing as the solution to the complex challenges present within these multistressed urban communities. A clearer examination of the ethical issues involved for initiating various reforms is warranted to help policymakers understand how their decision making will affect the future academic and employment opportunities of millions of underachieving students.

This chapter highlights the following social justice practices that can increase access to educational services for diverse student populations:

- Considering divergent perceptions on doing the right thing
- Reducing prejudice and discrimination through social justice
- Considering social justice in relation to resources

■ CONSIDERING DIVERGENT PERCEPTIONS

Several ethical issues must be discussed when considering student access to appropriate educational services. The first issue concerns defining how a teacher can provide appropriate services in an urban and economically challenged community. Wolf (1983) argues that good teachers do their best with the available material to help students develop their skills at a level that is relative to their abilities. When considering the economic disparities of facilities and resources available to teachers in some urban and multistressed communities, it is difficult to envision how teachers can adequately educate their students under the following conditions:

- The school plant and classrooms are aging and are not adequately heated, ventilated, repaired, or maintained.
- The classrooms lack adequate equipment, technology, and supplies.
- The teachers do not have textbooks for each student and many of the textbooks and resources are outdated or inappropriate for the students being served.
- The teachers lack adequate training, experience, or mentorship guidance to support the unique learning needs of their student community.
- Large percentages of teachers at the school site are still taking courses to clear their teaching credentials beyond the traditional school day and have limited time to adequately prepare for students' needs.
- The school site administrators lack adequate resources and skilled staffing to support teachers, students, and their families.
- The school site administrators are overwhelmed with the multistressed needs of their students and teachers.
- The school district is overwhelmed with trying to meet the needs of multistressed schools and becomes inefficient and bureaucratic in processing payroll requests, purchase orders, distributing supplies, collecting and distributing testing data, providing staff training and support, and conducting day-to-day business.

- Large percentages of parents are not literate and many have limited fluency in English.
- The parents have limited skills and knowledge in how to adequately support their children's learning needs.
- Many parents have limited experience with the American school system or with formalized classroom learning.
- Some of parents are or have been incarcerated and often lack adequate skills in providing basic needs for their children.
- Large percentages of students and their families live below the poverty level in overcrowded, multifamily substandard living arrangements.
- Large percentages of students do not live with a biological parent because the parent has a drug abuse problem or is incarcerated.
- Large percentages of students live in out-of-home placements or with a relative.
- The school and community have multiple challenges in maintaining a safe and secure environment due to gang violence and overall crime.
- The school and community lack adequate health and human care services to support the multistressed needs of community members.

When considering the unique educational needs of these students and their families, a second ethical issue remains. How can teachers best (a) respond to the social and economic inequalities among these students, (b) arrange educational experiences that are reasonably advantageous for all, and (c) provide educational experiences that allow equal access for all (MacKinnon, 2001)? Often, multistressed and urban school communities compensate for the variability of student needs by applying for and receiving funding that is designed to serve underperforming schools. Although many prescriptive programs have been created to address the needs of challenged school communities, many underperforming schools struggle with program implementation. This is partly because of the overwhelming daily survival stresses imposed on the school's principal and teacher leaders at that site.

In their efforts to address these obstacles, schools must cope with several interrelated issues. First, as schools attempt to implement various reforms designed to improve student learning, they must often cope with limited or flat funding support from their district or state. Second, the schools must also find ways to effectively evaluate program performance and replace ineffective programs with ones that work in their individual settings.

Historically, schools have not been effective in evaluating what specific strategies and reforms have produced the greatest impact on their multistressed students. Without a mechanism for identifying effective reform practices, there appears to be no magical way to create incentives for high student achievement and a process for decision making that can adequately measure effectiveness against costs (Hanushek, 1994).

When working with diverse groups of students, how does a teacher or a school site administrator determine what the best instructional practices should be for students who are second-language learners compared with students who have had poor academic preparation, or when considering students with special needs? When one reviews the demographic makeup of most urban and multistressed school communities, it is not uncommon for teachers to make daily determinations on how they can best modify their curriculum and instructional strategies to meet the greatest need of the largest number of students in their classroom. If a teacher approaches learning to serve the largest number of students, the principle of equality can be challenged by unjustly treating people differently in ways that deny some significant social benefits (MacKinnon, 2001).

The principle of social justice can best support discrepancies in a teacher's modification of instructional strategies to meet the greatest needs of his or her students. In application, social justice advocates that the teacher is justified in treating subgroups of students differently in socially acceptable ways if the teacher can prove that certain differences exist (MacKinnon, 2001). In the presence of students with widely diverse learning needs, educational treatments can at best appear dysfunctional in treating individual student needs differently in order to holistically serve their needs (Gordon, 1999).

Figure 2.1 provides a sample school site evaluation of current classroom strategies to meet diverse students' needs. Figure 2.2 includes a worksheet for principals and teacher leaders to brainstorm solutions on various strategies teachers can use in their classroom for increased adaptability and productivity in meeting unique student needs.

◼ REDUCING PREJUDICE AND DISCRIMINATION THROUGH SOCIAL JUSTICE

Social justice in schools means all students are entitled to the same rights and services. Social justice demands the elimination of prejudice and discrimination. Prejudice is an attitude of a closed mind or of one that is closed off to new ways of seeing beyond a stereotypical image. Prejudicial action that limits another group from exercising its constitutional or human rights is an act of discrimination and a denial of equality. Social justice programs in schools include activities that support a common goal of eliminating prejudice and discrimination based on race, color, national origin, and language background.

The patterns of racial, ethnic, nationality, language-background, and group relations in schools are developed by the way group members have been included or excluded within the society at large. A school's principal and teacher leaders should consider the present-day relationships of various student groups and include the history of exclusion for specific cultural groups. Informational programs should consider the following topics that may relate to specific cultural groups attending a school:

- The history of slavery
- The conquests of Native Americans and Mexican Americans
- Acts of discrimination against southern European immigrants
- The World War II relocation camps for Japanese citizens, including U.S. citizens of Japanese ancestry
- The experiences of Southeast Asian refugees

Figure 2.1. Sample Evaluation of Classroom Practices to Meet Student Needs

Teacher and Classroom Characteristic	*Teacher's Classroom Practices and Access to Services*
Overall layout	The classroom is set up with small learning centers for the teacher and community volunteers to assist students.
Layout of desks	Desks are clustered into cooperative learning centers to encourage students to peer tutor each other in project-based learning experiences.
Equipment availability	The classroom has a resource library with books, science experiments, social studies units, and language exercises.
Technology access	A technology leaning center provides students with access to computers, audiovisual equipment for tapes, and a digital camera to record leaning experiences.
Access to supplies	The students save projects on compact disks and have access to performing arts materials to support project development.
Textbook availability	All students have their set of textbooks and can check out a set for home use.
Supplementary resources	Businesses donate a variety of art supplies, computer educational software, digital camera supplies for reproducing photos, educational audiotapes, and videotapes.
Adequate training	The community and parent classroom volunteers receive six weeks of tutorial training and participate in ongoing staff development sessions with the teacher at the school.
Mentorship support	All students have a business mentor who visits them weekly in their classroom. Nearly 50% of the students participate in off-site monthly mentorship activities at the workplace. The teacher has a career advisor from the local state college.
Supplementary educational training	The teacher attends courses at the local state college to complete a master's degree in multicultural learning.

(Continued)

Figure 2.1. Continued

Teacher and Classroom Characteristic	Teacher's Classroom Practices and Access to Services
Administrative support	The school principal observes the teacher monthly and provides feedback on instructional strategies and access to other materials to enhance teaching.
Student accommodations for: Limited-English proficient (LEP) Low-income Out-of-home placements Special needs Underachieving	The school provides extra tutorial services to LEP and underperforming students before and after school. Low-income students participate in an after-school family literacy and career development program for students and their families. Out-of-home placement students who live in foster care homes participate in a daily after-school Big Brothers/Big Sisters Mentoring Program with community volunteers. Special needs students participate in an extensive career development training program at a sheltered work environment after school.
School and classroom safety	The school and all classrooms have safety procedures and policies for all emergencies and to ensure the safety and security of all children.
Parent and community support	The school has an extensive parent and community volunteer training, career development, and recognition program.

- The lives of political refugees from war-torn El Salvador and other countries
- Recent immigrants from Mexico and Latin America
- The conflicts within and between racial and ethnic minority groups
- Prejudices within a Hispanic cultural group and recent immigrants
- Conflicts and tensions between recent African and black Caribbean immigrants and domestic African Americans
- Tensions between Asian Americans and recent Asian immigrant populations

Historically, schools have been instrumental in helping newcomers adjust to this society. Schools continue to serve as the most prominent social institutions that support the adjustment of immigrants, migrants, and refugees to a new home. As resources become scarcer, more cultural

Figure 2.2. Brainstorming Worksheet to Increase Teacher Adaptability

Teacher and Classroom Characteristic	Teacher's Proposed Classroom Practices and Access to Services
Overall layout	
Layout of desks	
Equipment availability	
Technology access	
Access to supplies	
Textbook availability	
Supplementary resources	
Adequate training	
Mentorship support	
Supplementary educational training	
Administrative support	

Student accommodations for:
   Limited-English-proficient
   Low income
   Out-of-home placements
   Special needs
   Underachieving	

School and classroom safety	
Parent and community support	

communities will increase their competition for resources, attention, and power. Students in multiethnic and multiracial schools may also resegregate themselves from each other and seek out special places on the schoolyard to develop grassroots criteria for ethnic group membership. Schools may also contribute to resegregation. Culturally nonresponsive tracking practices may result in segregating students into honors classes, college preparatory tracks, regular or mainstream classrooms, and vocational and remedial classes. If these practices are culturally insensitive, they may create racially or ethnically homogeneous groupings that intensify existing stereotypes and discriminatory practices.

Ethnic, nationality, language, or racial identification can help students feel a sense of belonging. This identification, however, can also inhibit socially just interethnic contact and communication. Ethnic, nationality, language, or racial group membership can lead to the social exclusion of groups from friendships and social activities, and inhibit their status and popularity. Lack of contact can lead to conflict between these groups and will foster an alternative source of identification within the school. If culturally insensitive grouping practices occur in schools, they may lead to minority students being disproportionately assigned to a lower social status or lower course offerings, or having limited access to honors and college preparatory experiences. These socially unjust schooling practices can lead to social segregation that excludes minority groups from meaningful experiences with dominant group members and other minority groups. To respond to this challenge, schools must take the following actions:

1. Prevent ethnic, nationality, language, or racial group formations that impede academic progress.

2. Recognize that intergroup contact is likely to be the most effective means of reducing prejudice and discrimination.

3. Provide cultural and economic groups with the same relative status.

4. Have a common goal for all student groups.

5. Foster closer relationships among diverse student groups so students can respond to each other as individuals instead of members from another group.

Prejudicial attitudes and discriminatory behaviors will be reduced if the following conditions are met:

- Contact should be between members of relatively equal status. Frequent contacts between students and teachers are not likely to reduce prejudices between student groups. Students from different groups working to pass an examination might fulfill the equal status requirement.

- Contact must also be close and personal. Taking a field trip on the same bus may meet the equal status condition, but if the students do not talk to each other to foster some type of intimacy, there will be no reduction in prejudice. If students from different groups study together, prejudice will not be reduced if students limit themselves only to the subject matter they are studying. They must exchange personal information.

- Goals must be common goals. Achieving a goal requires the cooperation and resources of everyone.
- If groups interact with each other on an equal status basis to achieve common goals, students are more likely to understand that they are very much like each other. The more students believe that they are very much alike, the more difficult it is to be prejudiced against others.
- Students must be shown that prejudice, stereotyping, and discrimination violate the democratic values of equal opportunity and fair treatment. Prejudice is likely to be minimized when school personnel and students vehemently condemn prejudices like racism, ageism, and sexism. When the school norms against various forms of prejudice and acts of discrimination are visibly prominent, prejudice and discrimination can be reduced.

Other interventions to reduce prejudice and discrimination in schools are also essential, including educational approaches, vicarious experiences, and cooperative learning. These interventions will vary depending on the age of the students (McLemore & Romo, 1998).

Educational approaches are based on providing accurate information about other groups. The idea is that when accurate information is provided, there are fewer opportunities for stereotypes, and therefore, prejudicial attitudes based on lack of information to arise. This approach requires that teachers and students examine the contributions of various ethnic, racial, nationality, and immigrant populations to the development of this country. But it also requires the examination of the politics of exclusion and inequalities with respect to different ethnic, racial, nationality, language, and immigrant populations. When teachers and students gain more accurate knowledge about the life experiences of other groups, they are more likely to appreciate them and their families, communities, histories, and individual cultures. Drawing attention to the process of exclusion and discrimination, especially through team-building or cooperative learning activities, provides a foundation for developing a culture of tolerance and mutual understanding.

In addition to direct teaching about different groups in our society, students can engage vicarious approaches to learning about differences. Vicarious learning is based on the idea that beliefs are often acquired through observations and interpretations. Educational programs can use films, plays, novels, biographies, community speakers, and local community field trips to present materials and experiences of different groups. Emphasis should be placed on recognizing commonalities and reducing stereotyping. Principals and teacher leaders must reinforce tolerance for individual differences.

Cooperative learning is another strategy to promote intergroup interaction, tolerance, and mutual understanding. The idea behind cooperative learning with students of different backgrounds is to work together as a group to improve each member's academic accomplishments. Rewards, recognitions, or evaluations are not based on individual performance but on how a group promotes each member's performance. Intense interpersonal contact among members from different backgrounds is possible through cooperative learning activities. Caution should be taken to ensure that every student is provided an opportunity to contribute to a group. Positive racial/ethnic attitudes, intergroup friendships, improved scholastic performance, and significantly reduced stereotyping can be achieved through cooperative learning. When students work cooperatively they have increased opportunities to judge other students on their merits rather than on stereotypes or group memberships.

■ CONSIDERING SOCIAL JUSTICE IN RELATION TO RESOURCES

The concept of serving the greater good for the majority can empower students to achieve to their fullest potential and gain entry into four-year colleges for adequate career preparation. Adapting research conducted by Pablo Freire (1985) on transformational education; Marian Wright Edelman (1999) on community mentorships; Joel Spring (1998) on educational opportunity; and Jeannie Oakes, Karen Hunter Quartz, Steve Ryan, and Martin Lipton (2000) on civic virtue in educational reform, has produced the following ten tenets for student empowerment:

1. Institutional support: The school must provide institutional support embedded in social networks that provide attachments to individuals as "institutional agents." These individuals have the capacity and the commitment to provide and negotiate educational and community resources, support, and opportunities.

2. Social capital: The students must have access to social relationships and networks derived through the institutional support. Students must be encouraged to rely on the social capital and strengths they have as a group to collaborate and cooperate to succeed in college and encourage the success of future generations.

3. Mentoring: The students must be placed with a more capable peer group while engaging in an academic task and where they can learn from experienced mentors with respect to their career development.

4. Additive caring and cultural sensitivity: The school must provide institutional support, cross-cultural support, and social resources that build on each student's home and community experiences and promote bilingualism, biculturalism, and binationalism.

5. Programmatic interventions: The school must provide programs at all levels that enable students to navigate the higher education system. Examples include fast-start programs, pre-articulation programs, precollege academic socialization boot camps, high school/community college co-enrollment programs, and community college/four-year college co-enrollment options.

6. Career and vocational development: The school must integrate strategies into its curriculum that orient students on corporate America's occupational and vocational structure. Workforce preparation programs and school-to-work initiatives provide students with citizenship, business, and nonprofit organizational experiences through workplace paid apprenticeships, volunteer internships, and job shadowing programs.

7. Integrative civic virtue socialization: The school must provide institutional support to the students' families and community to ensure all students can adequately balance their family, community, work, and school obligations. Effective support mechanisms include parent education with child care, family literacy and employment skill development programs, pooling of school and community resources, and flexible scheduling of community support programs.

8. Public celebrations for accomplishments: The school must provide institutional support in celebrating diversity and student accomplishments through award banquets, newsletters, certificates of awards, special graduation ceremonies, and other activities that articulate the culturally responsive norms of the school's diverse student population.

9. Affirmation of ethnic and cultural differences: The school must provide institutional support and ethnically responsive and culturally sensitive interventions for students and their families who are political refugees and immigrants from other countries. School interventions should include an appropriate orientation to the American school system that will help students and their families incorporate the culturally rich American heritage into their daily lives.

10. Social justice and the democratic process: The school must provide institutional support in developing programs that foster a meaningful engagement with diverse student populations on social justice and the democratic process. This engagement can contribute to critical changes in a school's practices that can further promote student achievement. Students can have opportunities to acquire democratic values through citizenship education. Citizenship education can help students resolve the inequities of racism, classism, and sexism, and develop democratic ideals that reflect the needs, hopes, dreams, and realities of all citizens (Banks, 1997). Community service projects can be designed to supplement this curriculum and respond to the needs of a community while advancing the academic goals of students (Boethel, 1999).

Figure 2.3 provides a sample ten tenets for student empowerment self-assessment. Figure 2.4 provides the school's principal and teacher leaders with a self-assessment worksheet that can be used for developing strategies that support these ten tenets for student empowerment.

Figure 2.3. Sample Ten Tenets for Student Empowerment Self-Assessment

Student Empowerment Tenet That Ensures School and Career Success	Description of the School's Programs and Practices That Support This Tenet
1. Institutional support	The school provides students with cultural diversity and conflict resolution training. The school networks and collaborates with various cultural communities for cultural sensitivity training, curriculum units, cultural community celebrations, and culturally relevant resources.
2. Social capital	The students meet with local colleges for career advising and college preparation.
3. Mentoring	Students mentor each other in the classroom. Business volunteers mentor students in the classroom and provide career guidance and job shadowing at the workplace.
4. Additive caring and cultural sensitivity	Parents and cultural community leaders are invited to the school to share their culture with students in project-based learning activities. Students create a book about their family heritage based on these visitations.
5. Programmatic interventions	Local colleges provide students and their parents with career guidance seminars at the school. Students attend precollege sports camps, performing arts clinics, computer technology training, and career development classes.
6. Career and vocational development	Students learn the relevance of accounting and finance in their math coursework. Students are taught how to create a resume, and basic research project development skills during the language arts period. Students apply their academic vocational development skills in a community-based service learning project.
7. Integrative civic virtue socialization	Students are taught how to balance various aspects of their home and school life in their social studies units. Parents participate in parent education classes on how to nurture the developmental growth and academic needs of their children.

Student Empowerment Tenet That Ensures School and Career Success	*Description of the School's Programs and Practices That Support This Tenet*
8. Public celebrations for accomplishments	The school sponsors a monthly student recognition event and provides students with awards for outstanding attendance, outstanding academic performance, academic improvement, outstanding citizenship, and community service.
9. Affirmation of ethnic and cultural differences	Teachers provide students and parents from other countries with weekly orientation meetings on the American school system and how to access community resources. Parents and students are also taught about the American laws pertaining to domestic violence, dating, drug and alcohol usage, and citizenship.
10. Social justice and the democratic process	The school provides monthly assemblies for students and staff on social justice practices. Teachers participate in ongoing staff development sessions on how to create learning environments and curriculum units that support social justice and the democratic process. Students are taught how to respect and value the uniqueness of each student's cultural heritage.

Figure 2.4. Ten Tenets for Student Empowerment Self-Assessment

Student Empowerment Tenet That Ensures School and Career Success	Description of the School's Programs and Practices That Support This Tenet
1. Institutional support	
2. Social capital	
3. Mentoring	
4. Additive caring and cultural sensitivity	
5. Programmatic interventions	
6. Career and vocational development	
7 Integrative civic virtue socialization	
8. Public celebrations for accomplishments	
9. Affirmation of ethnic and cultural differences	
10. Social justice and the democratic process	

3

Building Partnerships for Educational Equity

Many students of urban and underperforming schools feel hostility from uncaring institutions (Valenzuela, 1999). In addition, most academic content courses do not consider the relevance of a student's socioeconomic and cultural background and their meaningful ties to learning (Spring, 2000; Valenzuela, 1999). Few universities and colleges are sensitive to these conditions in urban and culturally diverse schools. Most continue to insist that all schools produce evidence of conformity to specific high school content areas regardless of whether the curriculum is challenging and can adequately prepare students for scoring competitively on college entrance exams. Based on these conditions, students feel overwhelmed when having to overcome and compensate for the inadequacies and injustices within these schools (Valenzuela, 1999).

To respond to these inadequacies, urban and multistressed schools should modify their course content and course offerings to provide the information required for students to have access to any occupation or any social class (Spring, 2000). Many urban and multistressed school districts respond to these inadequacies by creating magnet, alternative, charter, and public schools of choice. These alternative schools create specialized programs that provide students with experiences and academic preparation for specific career development in performing arts, technology, engineering, medicine, community services, or business. Conditions for the effective educational development of these programs include the following (Gordon, 1999):

- A supportive organizational structure
- Adequate human and curricular resources
- Quality teaching and learning opportunities
- An adequate sense of self and relatedness to others
- Positive learning attitudes and behaviors of students
- Family and community support for learning

Communities can become more participatory in responding to the needs of underperforming students by partnering with schools for the common good of the community (Oakes, Quartz, Ryan, & Lipton, 2000). Forming effective partnerships with schools can eradicate racial and economic disparities for students. By connecting schools with community members, parents can become reengaged in their students' leaning and have access to a variety of health and social services, teams of teachers and service providers, and educational and community advisory programs (Oakes et al., 2000). This ethical approach to a public school's development can contribute to caring communities beyond the classroom and into inner-city communities (Spring, 2000; Oakes et al., 2000). Involving diverse community stakeholders to support urban and multistressed schools can be achieved through the following strategies:

- Creating effective community relations
- Building problem-solving coalitions and task force groups
- Developing community relationships for resource procurement
- Creating visibility for leveraging resources
- Identifying how community agencies can be included in a school's programming
- Defining how businesses can support academic programming and delivery
- Creating a seamless delivery of educational services

■ CREATING EFFECTIVE COMMUNITY RELATIONS

Community relations in urban and multistressed school environments must consider the high unemployment levels, low job skills, poor housing, and diverse socioeconomic challenges of students' families. Urban school districts require community relations efforts that include the following components (Sanders, 1999):

1. Curricular changes that respond to the changing global economy and adequately prepare students for entrance into higher educational institutions

2. Reform efforts that incorporate site-based management and community support

3. Integrated multicultural and multiracial education that is responsive to diverse student needs

4. Safety programs that renew communities and deter violence

5. Alternative programs and services that are tailored to meet the unique learning needs of the community's students

Effective community relations programs in economically challenged communities require a proactive approach to responding to the community. These programs should provide timely information about the school district's delivery of services, administration, safety, student accountability, and performance measures. The school community's stakeholders should be notified when (a) a school or student has received an outstanding recognition to celebrate, (b) the school has received a significant donation, or (c) a volunteer has provided a significant contribution to the school community. Effective public relations activities in urban and multistressed school communities include the following:

- Ongoing publications produced by the school and school district informing parents, students, and community collaborators about their rights and responsibilities and how they can best serve each other in supporting student achievement
- Ongoing press releases, publications, newsletters, and radio and television communications on the efforts and successes of various stakeholder groups in supporting student achievement
- Quarterly community forums for key stakeholders to meet with the school's principal and teacher leaders to identify effective strategies for school improvement and to brainstorm solutions for ongoing community challenges that impede student achievement
- Planned culturally sensitive community celebrations showcasing the successes of the school and students in achieving program goals and academic accomplishments
- Awards ceremonies for outstanding achievement
- Planned opportunities to evaluate and make recommendations for change in all academic and supplementary program areas
- Planned opportunities to volunteer and support student achievement

Figure 3.1 provides a worksheet for school principals and teacher leaders to brainstorm an effective public relations program for their school site.

BUILDING PROBLEM-SOLVING COALITIONS AND TASK FORCE GROUPS ■

Developing meaningful community involvement in urban and multistressed communities requires that the school's principals and teacher leaders become open to change. School staffs must also provide a welcoming environment for diverse stakeholders to support the school's primary purpose of educating a community's children. Community-empowered schools should create policies and procedures that support community problem solving and the formation of task force groups. Schools that support community involvement should consider the following strategies (Burke & Picus, 2001):

- Maintaining a clean and orderly facility
- Providing a culturally responsive staff with effective bilingual support services

Figure 3.1. Public Relations Program Plan

Public Relations Program Component	Description of Your Current and Proposed Public Relations Activities
Informational pieces informing stakeholders of rights and responsibilities	
Press releases, publications, newsletter, radio and television communications	
Quarterly forums for school improvement	
Planned community celebrations	
Awards ceremonies	
Evaluations for existing programs	
Volunteer opportunities to support student achievement	
Other:	

- Providing students and families with supplemental services outside the classroom
- Creating a comprehensive stakeholder volunteer and resource development program

School site problem-solving coalitions and task force groups can be created through the following process:

1. The principal should assemble a school leadership team that is clear about its purpose to support a communitywide problem-solving process.

2. Leadership team members must agree on their roles and responsibilities.

3. The leadership team should identify meeting protocols, decision-making models, and determine appropriate feedback processes (WestEd, 1996).

4. The school's leadership team should conduct an internal needs assessment with teachers, staff, and students to identify obstacles in supporting students' academic achievement.

5. Once the school's leadership team identifies the school's specific needs and challenges, the team should organize a community meeting and invite the community's stakeholders to learn more about the school's current services and needs for development.

6. At the meeting a formal presentation can be made on the school's current programs and needs.

7. After the presentation, work teams of stakeholders can be established with a specific timeline to complete certain tasks.

8. Depending on the amount of work required to complete a specific activity, individual work teams may need to create a mission statement and a strategic work plan for solving multifaceted problems.

9. Occasionally, work teams are slow to respond to a defined need. All participants at the initial community meeting must be reminded that change takes time. Demanding expectations for immediate results can become overwhelming and deter stakeholders from staying committed to a work team (WestEd, 1996).

10. At the end of the meeting, all stakeholders should clarify their roles, responsibilities, and a timeline for completing individual activities. The anticipated outcomes should be defined and stakeholders must determine how they will measure their successes while achieving various outcomes.

11. A calendar of follow-up meeting dates, times, and locations should also be circulated at the community meeting to all participating stakeholders.

Although community relations and problem-solving strategies are central to the success of school organizations, urban and multistressed school communities must have the flexibility to redesign and restructure various educational components to better meet all prevailing political challenges (Sanders, 1999). Figure 3.2 provides an internal needs assessment for school leadership teams to use in identifying any emerging needs for a community task force or problem-solving coalition meeting.

■ DEVELOPING COMMUNITY RELATIONSHIPS FOR RESOURCE PROCUREMENT

Community partnerships with diverse stakeholders can assist urban and multistressed school communities in leveraging and securing funding and resources for new program development and program expansion. A community stakeholder's involvement in a school can provide the following services (Schmitt & Tracy, 1996):

- Enhance the K-12 curriculum and link resources from the community to academic content.
- Expand and improve the use of community facilities in the delivery of academic services.
- Provide added learning opportunities for youth and lifelong learning for adults.
- Deliver and coordinate school-linked services from community agencies.
- Contribute to the community stakeholders' involvement in the decision making of the school.
- Improve a community's support of schools and leverage more policy and financial support for public education.
- Add instructional programs and resources that can meet the career development of students.
- Increase staff development resources and expertise.

Schools can create results-focused and long-term community partnerships with diverse partners by clearly communicating the intent for forming the partnership. All key partnership stakeholders should be committed to serving the majority of students' needs. The school should formulate a strategic plan and structure for facilitating the partnership with a shared vision and common outcomes that can leverage resources, monitor progress, and overcome political turf issues (Sweeney, Schenirer, & Lefkovitz, 2001).

Strategies for developing effective collaborative school-linked services include the following (Olsen et al., 1994):

- Conducting an assessment of student needs and an analysis of current services available within the community
- Analyzing the appropriateness of services for various ethnic and linguistic communities
- Creating stakeholder forums to construct program delivery
- Providing communication channels and a timeline to discuss how this partnership can benefit individual groups
- Integrating program development with existing school services
- Identifying strategies that reward various stakeholders for effectively working together

Figure 3.2. Internal Problem-Solving Needs Assessment

In the right column describe the type of help your school would benefit from in resolving the need listed in the left column.

Need Category	Description of Need
Student demographics and data collection	
Facility development and maintenance	
Leadership and organizational support	
Classroom organization, equipment, technology, and supplies	
Teachers' experience, credentialing, and training	
Textbooks and curriculum support materials	
Student achievement	
Accommodations to meet students' individual needs	
Family and community support	
Resource development	

Schools can also encourage parents and community members to become actively involved in providing classroom support. The following activities can support the usage of various community volunteers in the classroom and at the school site (Burke & Picus, 2001):

- Developing cooperative learning environments for students and community members
- Involving community members to provide tutorial support
- Inviting community members to share their knowledge about various countries and cultural practices, workplace career options, science explorations, and performing arts activities
- Assisting teachers with academic curriculum development and student support activities
- Providing students with technology training to support academic research projects
- Creating performing arts units to support academic subjects

Figure 3.3 provides a worksheet for the school principal and teacher leaders to identify how they may obtain various types of services, funding, and resources to support their needs.

■ CREATING VISIBILITY FOR LEVERAGING RESOURCES

Urban and multistressed schools must consider how they can best leverage visibility to gain access to diversified and integrated funding sources. Alternative schools and schools that have successfully implemented effective reform initiatives have been instrumental in gaining the attention of the media to share their stories. Initially, these schools create public relations materials about their schools that can include the following:

- A publication on the history and development of the school's services and how students have performed academically in response to these activities
- Tee shirts, mugs, magnets, folders, day planners, and other resources with the mission of the school and a logo representing the school's mission and purpose
- Signage, posters, and murals displaying the school's logo, mission, and purpose throughout the school facility
- Bulletin boards in the main office and in heavy traffic areas that showcase the school's many accomplishments and include pictures of key visitors who have celebrated these accomplishments
- A display case of plaques, trophies, awards, and proclamations from local, state, and federal political leaders recognizing the school's many accomplishments

Once the school organizes the information about its many successes, the school's leadership team should create a strategic public relations campaign that will generate high visibility. The following ten strategies can effectively support schools in their public relations campaign:

(Continued on page 49)

Figure 3.3. School Resource Development Worksheet

Need Category	Specify the Types of Resources Required for Each Need Category
Student demographics and data collection	Types of grants and funding sources: Materials and equipment: Types of volunteers and services:
Facility development and maintenance	Types of grants and funding sources: Materials and equipment: Types of volunteers and services:
Leadership and organizational support	Types of grants and funding sources: Materials and equipment: Types of volunteers and services:
Classroom organization, equipment, technology, and supplies	Types of grants and funding sources: Materials and equipment: Types of volunteers and services:
Teachers experience, credentialing, and training	Types of grants and funding sources: Materials and equipment: Types of volunteers and services:

(Continued)

Figure 3.3. Continued

Need Category	Specify the Types of Resources Required for Each Need Category
Textbooks and curriculum support materials	Types of grants and funding sources: Materials and equipment: Types of volunteers and services:
Student achievement	Types of grants and funding sources: Materials and equipment: Types of volunteers and services:
Accommodations to meet students' individual needs	Types of grants and funding sources: Materials and equipment: Types of volunteers and services:
Family and community support	Types of grants and funding sources: Materials and equipment: Types of volunteers and services:
General resource development	Types of grants and funding sources: Materials and equipment: Types of volunteers and services:
Specify other:	Types of grants and funding sources: Materials and equipment: Types of volunteers and services:

1. Schools should develop ongoing relationships with various media sources and regularly submit press releases to these sources on the school's various activities, accomplishments, and changes.

2. Schools should establish relationships with policymakers and business leaders who can help the school access services and funding for various activities.

3. Schools should create a calendar of events that media and key community leaders can be invited to attend that will showcase students' achievements and accomplishments in various programs.

4. Students who demonstrate unique leadership skills and accomplishments should be recognized through human-interest media submissions and through special awards ceremonies.

5. Legislators, grant funders, and the media should be invited to funder recognition activities that showcase a grant's benchmark accomplishments.

6. If the media is not able to attend celebration events, the school's leadership team or district should take pictures to showcase historical public moments and display these pictures on bulletin boards and through other communications channels in the community.

7. The school's leadership team or district can sponsor guest speakers on important educational issues and invite community members and the media to attend the event. Guest speakers can be recruited from local universities that are conducting research on a particular educational issue. The school or district can also contact a state or national expert on a particular topic to leverage greater event visibility.

8. The school's leadership team or district can create an educational forum with the community's leaders and stakeholders on key educational initiatives and school reform activities that may have an impact on the community.

9. The school's leadership team or district can create a community problem-solving forum on school safety, educational reform strategies, or school-community relations.

10. The school's leadership team or district can sponsor a community fair that showcases a school's or district's various clubs, sports teams, or organized activities. Each student group participating in the fair could create a fund-raising activity of food sales, games, or services as part of the fair. Community public service groups and businesses can provide demonstrations of various services and activities. The neighboring community and media can be invited to participate in the event. Schools can link these events to holiday and cultural celebrations.

Figure 3.4 provides a public relations planning worksheet that the school's principal and teacher leaders can use to brainstorm various strategies they can use for greater public relations visibility. After reviewing the information collected on the brainstorming worksheet, the school's principal and teacher leaders can create a calendar of monthly activities provided in Figure 3.5.

Figure 3.4. Public Relations Planning Worksheet

List your school-based public relations activities in the space provided for each category.

Category	Public Relations Activities
School site publications including news-letters and brochures	
Promotional materials including tee shirts	
Signage, posters, and murals displaying the school's mission or purpose	
Bulletin boards designed for public relations located in key traffic areas	
Display case for awards and trophies	
Types of press releases for various media relations	
Identify policymaker and business leader relationships and planned activities	
Types of human interest stories for media submissions	
Types of funder recognition events to showcase benchmark results	
Types of pictures that must be taken for the media and for public relations activities	
Types of educational issues for guest speaker presentations	
Key educational initiatives and problem-solving issues for community forums	

Category	Public Relations Activities
Types of school-based fund-raising events that showcase school programs	
Types of community fairs and celebrations that showcase students and school programs	
Types of cultural events that can showcase specific school activities and clubs	
Types of community events that student groups can attend to showcase the school	
Types of statewide and national conferences and activities students can attend to showcase their leadership talents	
Types of university partnership activities for students and the school	
Types of community-based leadership conferences for student and school leadership participation	
Specify other types of state and national activity:	
Specify other types of state and national activity:	

Figure 3.5. Monthly Calendar of Public Relations Activities

List the various types of public relations activities that your school can complete in the monthly table below based on the information compiled in Figure 3.4.

Month	Types of Public Relations Activities to Increase Visibility
January	
February	
March	
April	
May	
June	
July	
August	
September	
October	
November	
December	

HOW COMMUNITY AGENCIES CAN BE ■
INCLUDED IN A SCHOOL'S PROGRAMMING

School-community partnerships have significantly increased in recent years with curriculum that include experiential learning, an expanded content, and real-world exposure (Schmitt & Tracy, 1996). Community partnership activities can be provided at the school site. This communities-in-schools type of activities integrate education, health, and human care services into the school's daily program, or provide services at the school site as part of an extended program. Schools can also join forces with universities that conduct community-based research and develop new products in response to this research.

An example of this type of partnership may include an inner-city school partnering with a local university to receive tutorial support training through a federally funded AmeriCorps literacy project. Dental services can be provided to students and families through the university's dental school. Health and human care services can be managed through the university's school of social work and provided by the university's medical school. Innovative educational strategies and staff development services can be provided through the university's school of education. This integrative service delivery example can use the school as the hub of its neighborhood's revitalization efforts.

Community-based service learning projects can also support neighborhood revitalization efforts. Service learning projects can be designed to accomplish the following goals for students (Boethel, 1999; Schmitt & Tracy, 1996):

- Enhance academic achievement and program delivery
- Make learning relevant
- Build critical thinking skills
- Build character, leadership, and the ability to bring about positive change
- Foster citizenship and civic responsibility
- Increase altruism and compassion for others
- Increase self-esteem
- Provide positive role models and career mentors
- Provide relevant work experiences and career exploration

Effective service learning projects include structured activities integrated into the school's curriculum. They are collaborative in their planning, program design, and evaluation process. Reflective activities are part of the planning, program implementation, and evaluation process. The collaborative process includes (a) defining the community's demographic profile, (b) brainstorming neighborhood assets and needs, (c) meeting with community members and agencies to research a community problem and establish program goals, and (d) creating a final product documenting the service or research. Figure 3.6 provides a worksheet for the school's principal and teacher leaders to define the neighborhood needs of their school's families and propose service learning activities to support those needs.

Figure 3.6. Service Learning Needs Assessment

Define Your School's Families' Neighborhood Needs	Describe Service Learning Projects That Can Respond to These Needs and Support Students' Academic Learning

DEFINING HOW BUSINESSES CAN SUPPORT ACADEMIC PROGRAMMING AND DELIVERY

School-to-work strategies are designed to increase students' educational and career opportunities by encouraging business partners to help students make the connection between what they learn in the classroom and specific workplace skills (Fitzgerald, 1997). Students can acquire workforce preparation through school-based career awareness and training, through a planned work-based job training program, or by coordinating activities between the school-based and the worked-based program components (Schmitt & Tracy, 1996). Effective rules for developing partnerships include (a) setting realistic timelines for program planning and development, (b) expanding effective community-based programs, (c) reaching consensus with all stakeholders on the program's goals and objectives, and (d) minimizing conflict to retain healthy relationships (Fitzgerald, 1997). The following ten business partnership opportunities can provide significant benefits to students (Comer, Ben-Avie, Haynes, & Joyner, 1999; Fitzgerald, 1997):

1. Students will gain an understanding of what is required for high-skill careers to adequately prepare for advanced educational training.

2. Students can gain high-skill work experiences that will prepare them for future employment.

3. Students can participate as employed student apprentices and interns to generate an income in addition to career exploration.

4. Businesses can pay students tuition and fees for higher learning opportunities.

5. Students can attend guest speaker presentations with business leaders, participate in business conferences, and go on field trips to industrial facilities.

6. Students can receive technologically advanced equipment from local businesses to support their career development objectives.

7. Students can shadow industry leaders at their work sites for career development.

8. Students can work with industry leaders in creating various products and strategies for the community.

9. Students can participate in marketing focus groups and business forums to evaluate new product development.

10. Students' classrooms can support new product development by serving as beta test sites.

School-to-work programs can create new opportunities for students' professional growth and provide access to various vocational education programs. School districts can negotiate contracts and place students in career development programs and vocational training to support local businesses. Business support services can include manufacturing support, printing, editing, mailing, accounting and financial support services, inventory control, health and human care support services, academic tutoring services, child care services, and youth development programs. High schools can also support the local chamber of commerce by allowing students to conduct economic development needs assessment surveys (Blakely, 1997). In addition to providing critical economic services to their communities, these programs can support employers' recruiting, referring, and placement efforts (Fitzgerald, 1997). Figure 3.7 provides a business partnership needs assessment for the school's principal and teacher leaders to identify needs that can effectively be served through a school-business partnership.

■ CREATING A SEAMLESS DELIVERY OF EDUCATIONAL SERVICES

Once schools become skilled at working with diverse community service learning partners and school-to-work business partners, they can learn to create a seamless delivery of ongoing services that can adequately support the diverse cultural, ethnic, and socioeconomic needs of their urban and multistressed communities (Burke, 2002). The combination of integrative services that can be coordinated can be extensive. For example, one inner-city youth development agency can provide career exploration and mentoring programs to all of its program youth. The program's core services can include after-school child care, recreational and sports activities, performing arts, tutorial support, gang intervention and counseling, alternative educational programs, healthy meals, and mentorship services that provide students with the support necessary to achieve their personal dreams. The youths' families can attend parent education classes and receive basic need support services. When considering the diverse services of this community center example, it is apparent that the educational, health, human care, and economic development needs of the community can determine what specific services the agency will provide its youth at any given time.

Besides working with multiple businesses, community agencies, and industries, all alternative education programs can be managed through the local public school district. When considering the outreach examples described in this chapter, community agencies can develop school-based satellite programs throughout a community to increase service access. Figure 3.8 provides a matrix worksheet of service options that a school's principal and leadership team can use to create their school-based programs with community agencies and businesses.

Figure 3.7. Business Partnership Needs Assessment

Define Your School's Needs	*Describe the Business Projects That Can Respond to the School's Specific Needs*

Figure 3.8. Matrix Worksheet of Community and Business Service Options

List Type of Services That Your School's Families Would Benefit From at Your School Site	*Describe the Community Agency Services That Can Be Provided at Your School Site*	*Describe the Business Services That Can Be Provided at Your School Site*
Educational and career development services		
Parent education and student academic support		
Family counseling		
Medical, dental, and vision services		
Specify service:		
Specify service:		
Specify service:		
Specify service:		

4

Shortcuts for Accessing Critical Resources

As students' needs increase, the effective use of school resources is critical for promoting student performance (Burtless, 1996; Ladd, 1996). Integrative social services offered at neighborhood schools can maximize students' academic and social development. These collaborative service systems can reduce fragmented and duplicated support services. Effective community collaborations can provide site-based educational enrichment, health, social services, and mental health services. These programs can be flexible, preventative, family-focused, and child-centered (Karasoff, 1999). They can also help families develop effective life skills to increase basic survival and employment opportunities (Fitzgerald, 1997; Kerchner, 1997).

The following chapter sections describe how these collaborative partnerships can meet the diverse needs of disparate student groups:

- Identifying resource availability and funding options
- Researching and brainstorming program development options
- Brainstorming solutions for accessing resources

IDENTIFYING RESOURCE ■ AVAILABILITY AND FUNDING OPTIONS

Most urban schools qualify for numerous state and federal funding entitlements and grants. Urban schools are often contacted by community-based agencies and businesses to form grant development collaborations. How an urban school responds to these opportunities can critically affect its daily operations. Building effective coalitions requires the following considerations:

1. Before a school becomes a member of a coalition, the designated school representative should determine why the coalition is being formed and what benefits will be gained for the students.

2. If the coalition has been formed to plan a program for a grant, the grant's policies, procedures, and legislation should be reviewed to determine if the school should apply for funding alone or join a partnership for better outcome results.

3. When the school becomes a member of a coalition, a team of appropriate representatives from the school should be selected to attend the initial coalition meeting.

4. At the coalition meeting, the roles of each coalition partner should be defined. A coalition partner's historical background, current programs, and funding should be summarized. The coalition's leader can design a questionnaire to collect information that will be necessary for the program planning or funding. Questionnaires can include the students' demographics, academic performance, attendance rates, suspensions, expulsions, crime data, and a summary of the students' and school's needs. The coalition may create a program plan with goals, objectives, timelines, and evaluation instruments. Surveys should be completed to identify the needs of all stakeholder groups (Burke, 1999). Letters of support or memorandums of understanding may be required from a school to document its community support. Figures 4.1, 4.2, and 4.3 contain samples of a demographic questionnaire for several schools, an individual school's program plan, and a school-based needs assessment survey.

5. A designated representative should advise the appropriate decision makers if the school site will fully commit itself to the coalition's plan of action.

6. Some school districts informally ask the superintendent to support the coalition's grant development. Most school districts have the fiscal or business office and the superintendent review the entire grant packet for submission. These districts may also have a form for all reviewers to sign that indicates their approval for coalition involvement.

As urban schools receive more coalition requests from the community, the need for a formalized approval process is critical. Figure 4.4 provides a sample school district approval form that can be used to organize a coalition of stakeholders to create a school site program or to write a program grant.

■ RESEARCHING AND BRAINSTORMING PROGRAM DEVELOPMENT OPTIONS

Urban school districts receive ample opportunities to apply for funding from federal sources, state sources, local sources, and businesses because

Figure 4.1. Sample School District Demographic Questionnaire

Complete the table of data characteristics for each school in the coalition.

School Characteristics	School A	School B	School C	School D
Number of students enrolled				
% of white students enrolled				
% of black students enrolled				
% of Hispanic students enrolled				
% of Asian students enrolled				
% of Native American/ Alaskan students enrolled				
% of low-income students				
% of students qualifying for free lunches				
% of limited-English- proficient students				
Number of suspended students				
Number of expelled students				
Number of abuse referrals				
Number of counseling referrals				
Overall state standardized academic test results				
Names of business and community agency partners				

Figure 4.2. Sample School Plan to Increase Parent Involvement

List your school's program goals, objectives, timelines, and evaluation instruments in the spaces provided.

Goal	Objectives	Timeline	Evaluation
To increase family literacy and support students' achievement	By 6/XX, 80% of the students' parents will demonstrate effective questioning skills to reinforce reading comprehension.	2/XX through 6/XX	Observation and knowledge surveys
To recruit parents to participate in reading activities at the school site	By 6/XX, each classroom will have 10 trained parent volunteers working in each classroom to support reading activities.	2/XX through 6/XX	Log-in sheets, observations, and knowledge surveys
To recruit parents to serve on the school's advisory council	By 10/XX, each grade level at the school will have one designated parent attend the school's monthly advisory council meetings.	9/XX through 10/XX	Log-in sheets and interviews to document involvement
To recruit parents to write grants	By 1/XX, each grade level at the school will train a parent volunteer to assist with the school's grant-writing activities for program development.	10/XX through 1/XX	Grantwriting knowledge survey and completed grant

Figure 4.3. Sample School Needs Assessment Survey

Consider the following needs at your school and circle the appropriate numerical value (1 = *high* and 5 = *low*) to rate the highest needs for the following services:

	High				**Low**
1. Supplementary services to support student achievement	1	2	3	4	5
2. Before-school tutorial services	1	2	3	4	5
3. After-school tutorial services	1	2	3	4	5
4. Before- and after-school child care	1	2	3	4	5
5. After-school arts education classes	1	2	3	4	5
6. After-school clubs	1	2	3	4	5
7. After-school team sports	1	2	3	4	5
8. Family literacy training	1	2	3	4	5
9. Computer literacy classes for families	1	2	3	4	5
10. English-as-a-second-language classes	1	2	3	4	5
11. Translation services for parent conferences	1	2	3	4	5
12. Student and family counseling services	1	2	3	4	5
13. Medical care and immunizations	1	2	3	4	5
14. Dental care	1	2	3	4	5
15. Vision and hearing tests	1	2	3	4	5
16. Social services and basic needs	1	2	3	4	5
17. Legal and immigration services	1	2	3	4	5

Figure 4.4. Sample Program Coalition School District Approval Form

Program Originator:_____ Funding Cycle Dates:_____

Name of Proposed Program: _____

Briefly Describe the Program: _____

_____

_____

Name of Coalition Business or Community Agency	Description and Budget for Services to Be Provided Requiring Funding	Description and Value of Services to Be Donated

Proposed Fiscal Agent and Contact Name	Description and Budget for Services to Be Provided Requiring Funding	Description and Value of Services to Be Donated

Coalition Approval Signatures:

_____   _____
Fiscal Director's Signature   Date

_____   _____
Superintendent's Signature   Date

of their unique demographic needs. In response to these opportunities, school principals and teacher leaders must prioritize the most critical needs to be filled at their school site. If a school's leadership team decides to focus on increased family involvement as a primary need, the school's leaders can design their plan for parent recruitment, training, and participation at various school and community planning events (Burke & Liljenstolpe, 1992). When seeking funding to increase parent involvement at the school, the following strategies can ensure successful program development:

1. When a school applies for a grant, the grantwriter should contact the funder and attend the bidder's conference to learn more about the grant's development procedures.

2. Through the funder's recommendations, the grantwriter should visit currently funded projects to learn more about the program. During the project site visit, the grantwriter can ask the program coordinator for a copy of the project's grant to use as a program template. The grantwriter should also discuss any program implementation challenges with the program coordinator.

3. The grantwriter must consider program delivery options with various community agencies to determine who will provide specific program components and who will act as the program's fiscal agent.

4. The grantwriter must draft a memorandum of understanding for a proposed fiscal agent. Figure 4.5 includes a sample memorandum of understanding for a fiscal agent.

5. The grantwriter must prepare a grant template on all of the information he or she must obtain to complete the program plan and prepare for the stakeholder meeting. Critical information for the template may include an agency's demographic profile, its program history, the program goals and objectives, specific program activities with timelines, and measurable project outcomes that can be measured through various evaluation instruments. Figure 4.6 provides a sample program data collection template.

6. Through the input of the grant's stakeholders, the grantwriter should contact all prospective agency providers for contracted or donated services.

7. A prospective agency provider should be available to assist with all grantwriting activities at no charge and provide information to complete the grant request.

8. A prospective agency provider must submit a detailed budget, a program narrative, and any required supporting grant documentation before the grant deadline.

9. The school's principal and teacher leaders should only select prospective agency providers or business partners who can provide outstanding services and who are able to participate fully in the grant's development (Burke & Liljenstolpe, 1993).

Figure 4.5. Sample Fiscal Agent Memorandum of Understanding

January 15, 20XX

MEMORANDUM OF UNDERSTANDING BETWEEN THE SCHOOL AND THE COMMUNITY AGENCY FISCAL AGENT

To Whom This May Concern:

This Memorandum of Understanding confirms that this nonprofit community agency will serve as the project's fiscal agent and will be responsible for the following:

- All program and fiscal management activities

- All program and financial funder-reporting requirements

- All evaluation data collection, data analyses, and evaluation funder-reporting requirements

- All audits and other fiscal-reporting requirements designated by the funder

This letter also serves as a confirmation that the community agency will donate the following services at the school site for the principal and teacher leaders:

- Provide a three-day grant training course to a total of six participants valued at $500 per person × 6 participants = $3,000.

- Provide 20 hours of follow-up technical support to the six participants valued at $50 per hour × 20 hours = $1,000.

- The community agency will also send a representative to the school's monthly program development advisory meetings valued at $50 per hour × 18 hours = $900.

We look forward to acting as the fiscal agent and providing program support to the school's leadership.

The Agency's Executive Director's Signature

Figure 4.6. Sample Program Data Collection Template

Program Component	Types of Data Required and Strategies for the Program
Demographic overview	Student characteristics including total number of students and their ethnicity, students' standardized test results, the economic needs of students, supplementary service agencies, and needs assessment results
Need statement	A description and statistical analysis of an overall community need for the program and how this need relates to the specific school community to be served
Program goals	Broadly stated program goals that will be provided to the targeted student population in response to the need
Objectives with timelines and activities	A listing of measurable objectives that describe the actual services that will be performed within a given timeline and the activities that will be used to provide the services
Evaluation plan	Evaluation tools that will be used to measure the effectiveness and outcomes from the delivery of services
Staff's qualifications and organization's capacity	A description of the organization, the program staff's qualifications, the cultural relevancy of the staff, and the agency's experience working with the clients
Budget with diversified and future funding	Consideration of the program costs in relation to the number of clients to be served and the plans for diversified and future funding

10. When multiple agencies offer to provide similar program services, the grantwriter must select the appropriate partner for service delivery based on:

- The type of service that will be provided
- The experience of the agency and the staff in providing the service
- The cultural relevancy of the service to be provided for the demographic population to be served
- The cost effectiveness of the service to be provided when considering the number of clients to be served

11. The school's leadership should use customized community problem-solving grant templates to reduce the amount of time and effort in preparing the grant application. Grant templates can provide demographic information about the school's community, the school district's history, the school's demographics, and an overview of the program plan with goals, objectives, timelines, and evaluation instruments (see Figure 4.7 for a sample grant template).

12. When designing evaluation plans and instruments, the school's leadership team should consider the limitations of the school's capacity to track and evaluate data.

13. Evaluation instruments should be able to measure outcomes and identify changes in behaviors, attitudes, knowledge, and understanding.

14. Effective evaluation instruments can include interviews, focus groups, observations, journal documentation, log-in sheets, surveys, questionnaires, changes in behavior, increased academic performance, reduced absences, reduced counseling referrals, fewer crime incidents, and increased school retention. An increase in knowledge, attitude, or understanding can be measured through surveys and questionnaires. Behavior changes can be documented by observation and through behavior tracking journal entries and reflections.

15. Once funding is received, the school's principal or the designated fiscal agent's program director must contact the funder to adjust the program delivery plan according to changes that may have occurred before the program received funding.

■ BRAINSTORMING SOLUTIONS FOR ACCESSING RESOURCES

Community agencies can help schools provide students and their families site-based integrative health and human care services (U.S. Department of Education, 1994). Effective school partnerships with community agencies require a mutual respect, trust, and an ongoing exchange of the defined roles and responsibilities of each school partner (Burke & Picus, 2001). A school-based integrative service delivery system can include the following service components:

Figure 4.7. Sample Grant Template

Grant Component	How to Respond to Requested Information
Demographic overview	Describe the overall demographics of the community, the school district, the program schools, and student needs.
Need statement	Describe why this program is proposed with research citations and discuss how it will meet the needs.
Program goals	Provide broadly stated goals for the program.
Objectives with timelines and activities	Create objectives that are measurable within a specific timeline for a targeted group of students. Under each objective, list the activities that will support the objective outcomes.
Evaluation plan	Identify specific instruments that can be used for measuring program effectiveness.
Staff's qualifications and organization's capacity	Summarize the key qualifications of staff, and describe how the organization can support and accommodate the proposed program.
Budget with diversified and future funding	Describe how each budget item was derived and indicate other funding matches for the budget categories. Summarize the strategies for financially sustaining the project after funding has expired.

- Parent education on child development and academic support
- Mental health counseling for students and their families
- Domestic violence prevention training
- Employment development skill training including computer literacy
- Baby-sitting and child care certification training
- English-as-a-second-language training
- Basic subjects education and high school equivalency certification
- Academic mentorship and tutoring training to support student achievement
- Family literacy training
- Meal preparation and nutrition education
- First aid and safety training
- Basic needs support including housing assistance, food distribution, and clothing
- Immigration and legal assistance
- Case management support services
- Medical and dental services
- Hearing tests, vision examinations, and eyeglass distribution

When community agencies approach a school's principal to provide services, it is critical that the school's principal, with each community agency service provider, creates a memorandum of understanding (see Figure 4.8) that clarifies the roles and responsibilities of each stakeholder. The memorandum should also provide a detailed description of the services and donations to be provided. Any costs that will be incurred by the clients and the school site should be noted in the memorandum of understanding

Once the stakeholders sign the memorandum of understanding, monthly coordination meetings should be organized to evaluate the services being provided. School principals can combine monthly program evaluation meetings with their community's resource council meetings, Healthy Start collaborative meetings, or school and community relations committee meetings.

Business involvement in education can provide the following services (Ballan, Casey, & de Kanter, 1998; Burke & Picus, 2001):

- Supporting a community-based family literacy initiative
- Providing tutorial and mentorship literacy support in the classroom
- Training teachers in real-world mathematics applications
- Providing computers, Internet access, and computer literacy training to teachers, students, and families
- Providing service learning projects at work sites
- Supporting school-to-work community training programs and initiatives
- Establishing mentorship support to college-bound students and their families
- Providing college financial aide support and information to students and their families
- Sponsoring after-school child care, academic support, and sports clubs
- Encouraging employee participation at school sites through school adoption programs, volunteer release time, and release time for employees to participate at their child's school

Figure 4.8. Sample Donation Memorandum of Understanding

January 15, 20XX

MEMORANDUM OF UNDERSTANDING BETWEEN THE SCHOOL AND A COMMUNITY AGENCY DONATING SERVICES

To Whom This May Concern:

This Memorandum of Understanding confirms the support of the Community Grant Training Agency with the school's principal and teacher leaders. The Community Grant Training Agency is committed to donating effective grantwriting training to local schools and nonprofit community organizations. This letter serves as a confirmation that the Community Grant Training Agency will donate the following services to the school's principal and teacher leaders:

- Provide a three-day grant training course to a total of six school leaders valued at $500 per person $\times$ 6 participants = $3,000.

- Provide 20 hours of follow-up technical support to the six school leaders valued at $50 per hour $\times$ 20 hours = $1,000.

- The Community Grant Training Agency will also send a representative to the school's monthly community relations committee meetings valued at $50 per hour $\times$ 18 hours = $900

We look forward to providing ongoing support for the school's fund development needs.

The Agency's Executive Director's Signature

Besides providing computer equipment, teacher training, and employee release time to support schools, businesses are now partnering with schools in supporting their daily operations. Figure 4.9 provides a sample of the various business partnership services available at school sites.

Figure 4.9. Sample Business Partnership Services Provided at School Sites

Type of Business	Types of Services Provided
Accounting	Accounting firms can provide reduced fees for audits, monthly bookkeeping services, and supporting grantwriting activities.
Banking	Banks can help students open savings accounts and instruct students on how to manage their personal finances and credit.
Construction	Construction firms can provide supplies of scrap wood and other building materials for art projects and theater arts set design.
Restaurant	Restaurants can donate food for various fund-raising and community support activities and provide jobs to students.
Auto repair	Auto repair shops can donate cars and mechanics to train students on how to repair cars.
Beauty parlor	Beauty parlors can donate hair care products for various play productions and school benefit activities.
Florist	Florists can donate flowers for different school events and as recognition for students' performances.
Manufacturing	Manufacturing companies can donate marginal products for students to repair or use as a recyclable for an art project.
Stationery store	Stationery stores can donate office supplies to support a school's daily operations and fundraising donations.
Veterinarian	A veterinarian can donate animals for school visits and provide educational workshops about various animals.
Hospital	Hospitals can provide training in basic first aid and safety.

As parents, community agencies, and businesses formulate effective partnerships with schools, each stakeholder group can continue to develop innovative programs to meet emerging needs. Stakeholders must research emerging educational problems to identify effective problem-solving strategies and funding opportunities that will support new program development. Research should include studying similar programs that have been successful and understanding the policy-making process for enacting change (Burke & Picus, 2001). Stakeholders must also identify which specific educational leaders they should inform about a problem (Anderson, 1981).

Educational problem solvers should complete the following activities:

- Stakeholders should create informational brochures defining the educational need with proposed strategies to educate other stakeholders.
- Lobbyists can inform educational policymakers about the need for funding support.
- Funders must also be contacted to assist with funding.

Regardless of the strategies used to educate a school community about an educational problem, all stakeholders must create different strategies for equalizing the access and use of resources to meet the educational needs of disparate student populations (Fullan, 1993).

5

Evaluation Measurements That Ensure Equality

Program evaluation instruments must adequately evaluate economically challenged and culturally diverse students. An equitable educational assessment process should include the following strategies (Reeves, 2000; Gordon, 1999):

- Aligns with the school's incentives
- Considers the diversity of the students and individual schools
- Measures students' true abilities
- Meaningfully measures actual performance
- Specifies how teachers can help students understand what they are supposed to do
- Provides ongoing feedback for improvement
- Universally applies to all stakeholders' support for students' leaning
- Links content to students' learning experiences

This chapter provides sample evaluation templates that have the potential to authentically measure changes in students' academic performance. It also describes suggestions for further evaluation development that can integrate a student's academic performance with career options. A student's successful career preparation is dependent on the school's principal's and teacher leaders' response to overcoming academic deficiencies. Student evaluation measurements should consider the following topics:

- Defining academic outcomes for diverse student groups
- Creating a case management approach to evaluate students
- Considering accountability in relation to evaluations
- Measuring change using a continuous assessment plan

■ DEFINING ACADEMIC OUTCOMES FOR DIVERSE STUDENT GROUPS

Schools can increase students' academic outcomes and career preparation through the following strategies:

1. Limiting the tracking of students into particular career paths through student advising and academic performance grouping.

2. Providing relevant academic support and college eligibility information to students and their families with adequate accommodations for special needs families who work untraditional hours or who do not speak English.

3. Creating learning experiences that reflect the community's work ethic and needs.

4. Providing career development options for students including mentoring, internships, and job-shadowing programs.

5. Creating opportunities for parents and community members to have access to the school's academic programs for student support.

6. Using academic evaluation instruments to identify specific skills for job preparation, career development, and being informed citizens.

7. Enlisting the support of local businesses in school advisory councils to identify specific skills to meet the community's employment requirements.

8. Partnering with local colleges and universities to design academic outcome instruments that can authentically evaluate the skills required for various careers.

9. Educating teachers in how to create supportive letters of recommendation that can help students secure employment and access institutions of higher education.

10. Providing test preparation support to students on workplace testing requirements.

■ CREATING A CASE MANAGEMENT APPROACH TO EVALUATE STUDENTS

Fair and adequate testing of diverse student populations requires a case management approach for evaluating students' academic performance. First, the various stakeholders involved in the students' evaluation process must be identified. These may include the following stakeholder groups:

1. The school district's administrators must identify which assessment instruments can best meet the diverse needs of individual students and school sites.

2. School principals must provide feedback to their teachers on the various testing instruments that will be used to measure student achievement.

3. The state department of education must assist school sites in identifying appropriate test taking and reporting requirements to comply with the state's accountability system.

4. The test developers and manufacturers must be contacted to identify specific tests that can authentically measure specific student populations' academic achievement and to understand how to adequately prepare students and teachers for successful test completion.

5. The teachers must be trained in how to support students' skill development and how to adapt classroom curriculum and instructional strategies to meet students' needs.

6. The teachers must be trained on how to create a trusting classroom environment and engage students in the skills required for academic achievement.

7. The students must be trained on how to understand the content of a test.

8. Parents must be trained in how to support their students' academic achievement and interpret the testing data results.

9. Business leaders and community members must be educated on the various evaluation instruments and how they will affect students' career development.

All stakeholders must be educated in how to interpret test scores within a specific school community. Typically, low test score results in urban and multistressed communities have a negative impact on the neighborhood's overall growth. In addition, low test scores indicate that a school has not been able to meet the unique learning needs of specific ethnic, cultural, and economic classes of students. Lower test scores can also leverage significant financial resources to underperforming school sites. Categorical funders for underperforming schools typically describe specific consequences to a school if students' test scores do not sufficiently increase within a specific time period. Extreme consequences may include (a) the removal of a principal from a school site, (b) the state's takeover of an underperforming school, or (c) a transfer of an underperforming school to another school district. When all stakeholders collaborate in a case management approach to support student achievement, the school system can modify curriculum and instructional strategies to adapt to the individual needs of students.

■ MEASURING CHANGE USING A CONTINUOUS ASSESSMENT PLAN

An effective accountability system should be comprehensive in measuring test scores, attendance rates, dropout rates, student behavior, and entrance rates into four-year colleges. School district, school site, and community demographic data can provide a contextual or qualitative analysis of the environmental conditions that may effect a principal's or teacher leaders' ability to respond to students' academic achievement needs. Systemwide assessment indicators must adequately measure the achievement goals and objectives of the school district's students. Effective strategies for student test preparation and performance include the following (Gordon, 1999; Reeves, 2000):

1. Teachers must use diverse teaching, learning, and assessment strategies to meet individualized needs.

2. Teachers must be flexible in their time allocation for teaching various units and they should use multiple teaching strategies.

3. Teachers must provide students with procedural knowledge for learning.

4. Students should have the option to choose how they can best demonstrate what they have learned and how they can apply this conceptual knowledge to a finished product.

5. Students should be provided with a sociocultural perspective and indigenous experience samples to illustrate basic concepts.

6. Students should be provided with cooperative and project-based learning opportunities to apply basic concepts to real-life experiences.

7. Students should be respected and valued for their unique contributions in group and individualized learning experiences.

8. Students should have equitable access and inclusion in challenging learning and test preparation activities.

9. English language learners should have access to the instructional grade-level mainstream with adequate support services.

10. Resources should be equitably distributed to adequately meet and enrich the educational needs of diverse learners.

■ CONSIDERING ACCOUNTABILITY IN RELATION TO EVALUATIONS

Combining the existing student evaluation program with ongoing student evaluation strategies can help school principals and teachers better understand each student's academic growth and weaknesses. Analyzing information from a variety of sources provides teachers with the knowledge required for adapting curriculum for increased student performance.

Ongoing student evaluation strategies can help teachers determine if students have effectively integrated knowledge from the classroom to their home environment.

Some of the most effective reform strategies for underperforming schools include testing students on their basic subject knowledge every six weeks. Through the data collected on these ongoing diagnostic tests, school principals can temporarily shift students to remedial groups or to individualized tutorial sessions to respond to a student's demonstrated need for additional academic support. Inconsistencies can also be carefully examined by teachers to assure that students' instruction is appropriately challenging and will serve the best interests of the majority of the students. The following types of student assessment instruments can help school principals and teacher leaders design an effective plan for continuously evaluating the diverse needs of their students (Reeves, 2000):

- Observe and listen to students to gain insights about the verbal and nonverbal strategies they use to demonstrate their learning style and performance.
- Create an observational worksheet that identifies the degree of a student's demonstrated ability in completing specific tasks in a project (see Figure 5.1).
- Develop a checklist of competencies a student must demonstrate to measure his or her benchmark development in a specific academic subject (see Figure 5.2).
- Design performance evaluations that identify the frequency rate at which a student demonstrates specific learning behaviors during the completion of a project (see Figure 5.3).
- Create a matrix of concepts that will be used in a specific project and check off the concepts that were satisfactorily completed by various students (see Figure 5.4).
- Analyze a student's portfolio of writing samples, artwork, research reports, project-based learning products, and reflective journal process entries.
- Use portfolio assessment forms for each portfolio submission that include the objective of a specific activity, an assessment by the teacher, a process reflection from the student, and a student's justification for including this submission in his or her portfolio (see Figure 5.5).
- Use reflective journals to gain an understanding of what teaching strategies have contributed significantly to students' development.
- Use project-based learning activities and community service learning projects to apply educational concepts to demonstrated performances.
- Provide students with self-assessment surveys, behavior checklists, and attitudinal surveys to determine study skill development, learning experiences, and knowledge.
- Meet with students and caregivers to identify students' strengths, weaknesses, and their adaptability to apply newly learned knowledge in their home and community.
- Conduct focus groups with diverse stakeholder groups to gain knowledge about each group's perception on how students are achieving in their academic learning.

- Continuously analyze students' criterion-referenced and diagnostic testing results to identify the academic gains and challenges of individual students and classrooms.
- Evaluate students' demographic data, graduation requirements, report cards, and school records to identify any special circumstances that must be addressed in each student's daily program and make appropriate referrals to specialists for further evaluation or diagnostic testing.

Figures 5.1 through 5.5 provide sample assessment instruments that illustrate the types of evaluations described above. When using a specific assessment instrument with culturally and economically challenged groups of students, it is important to consider the contextual information that will be measured and how it relates to a student's prior learning experiences in his or her community and home environment. The impact of the evaluation must also be considered with regard to a student's selection and placement in particular programs, class groupings, and access to institutions of higher education.

Figure 5.1. Sample Student's Project Task Completion Observational Worksheet

Project Description: Each student will research on the computer various institutes of higher education and identify career preparation courses and programs at specific universities. Each student will write a letter of inquiry to an institute of higher education to learn more about a specific career option.

Student's Name: Rosa Hernandez

Project Task	*Degree of Demonstrated Ability*		
	Novice Attempted Effort	Apprentice Strong Capability	Novice Outstanding Application
Computer research	✓		
Data classification and assimilation		✓	
Writer's emotional expression in letter			✓
Letter's organizational construction			✓
Letter's sentence construction and language mechanics		✓	

Figure 5.2. Sample Student's Checklist of Competencies for Language Arts

Student's Name: Rosa Hernandez

Description of Competency (e.g., California Department of Education, 1992; Reeves, 2000)	Demonstrated Benchmark Date
Student can read and understand grade-level appropriate material.	9/10/XX
Student can confirm predictions about the text based on prior knowledge and through cues presented in the text.	12/15/XX
Student can write a few sentences about herself.	9/10/XX
Student can express ideas for a story with some support.	10/3/XX
Student uses some elements of organizing her thoughts to write a story independently.	11/18/XX
Student connects ideas and thoughts in writing with some sentence structure support.	1/4/XX
Student's expression reflects her emotional involvement.	3/26/XX
Student's story has a clear beginning, middle, and ending with limited support.	5/11/XX
Student's story has few mechanical, sentence structure, and spelling errors.	6/15/XX

Figure 5.3. Sample Student's Frequency Rate of Learning Behaviors Demonstrated Throughout Project Completion

Project Overview: Each student will research on the computer various institutes of higher education and identify career preparation courses and programs at specific universities. Each student will write a letter of inquiry to an institute of higher education to learn more about a specific career option.

Student's Name: Rosa Hernandez

Learning Behavior	Number of Times the Student Demonstrated the Learning Behavior During the Project's Duration		
	0 to 3 times	4 to 6 times	7 to 10 times
Independence while using the computer for research	✓		
Adequate research skills at specific Web sites		✓	
Ability to categorize, classify, and prioritize data		✓	
Ability to organize research and thoughts while constructing a letter of inquiry			✓
Writer's authenticity and reflective expression			✓
Letter's quality and mechanics		✓	

Figure 5.4. Sample Students' Project Matrix of Concepts Learned Checklist

In the worksheet below, list each student participating in a project-based learning experience. Check the level of concept completion for each student participating in the project.

Project Overview: Each student will research on the computer various institutes of higher education and identify career preparation courses and programs at specific universities. Each student will write a letter of inquiry to an institute of higher education to learn more about a specific career option.

Description of Project Concept	Student's Name	Satisfactory Completion	Needs Remedial Support
Demonstrated an understanding of how to conduct Web searches on university career and program options.	Rosa Charlie Miguel Harriet	✓ ✓ ✓	 ✓
Demonstrated effective computer research skills.	Rosa Charlie Miguel Harriet	✓ ✓ 	 ✓ ✓
Demonstrated curiosity and initiative.	Rosa Charlie Miguel Harriet	✓ ✓ ✓ ✓	
Organized data and information by categorizing and prioritizing.	Rosa Charlie Miguel Harriet	✓ ✓ ✓ ✓	
Drew logical conclusions from the results.	Rosa Charlie Miguel Harriet	✓ ✓ ✓	 ✓
Wrote a grammatically correct and comprehensive letter of inquiry.	Rosa Charlie Miguel Harriet	✓ ✓ 	 ✓ ✓
The letter reflected the writer's emotional involvement in the topic.	Rosa Charlie Miguel Harriet	✓ 	 ✓ ✓ ✓

Figure 5.5. Sample Student Portfolio Assessment Form

In the space provided, the teacher should describe the project objective for this portfolio submission.

By the end of the class period, the student will be able to write a letter of inquiry to an institute of higher education to learn more about the teaching credentialing career options and programs for bilingual students.

In the space provided, the teacher must summarize the student's performance in meeting the project objective.

Rosa did an outstanding job of identifying an appropriate institute of higher education that provides a variety of credentialing career options and programs. In her letter of inquiry, she was able to clearly articulate her interest in becoming a teacher and ask for career guidance on specific college preparation courses she should complete to become a bilingual teacher. Rosa succinctly explained her background and training in two languages and how she could use this training to assist other students in their academic achievement. Finally, Rosa exceeded the objective of this assignment by requesting financial aid information and a college admissions informational packet.

In the space provided, the student should summarize the learning process he or she engaged in to meet the project objective.

As an 8th grade student, I am becoming increasingly aware of how teachers who speak more than one language can really help limited-English proficient students improve their academic performance. When I first came from Mexico, my English speaking skills were limited. Most of my teachers could not speak Spanish and I had to rely on my classmates to understand my assignments. Since I learned how to speak adequate English, I am interested in helping other students become successful in the American school system. This is my reason for exploring a career as a bilingual teacher. I also know that it is not too soon to think about the required courses, the educational costs, and the teacher education program's college admissions process.

(Continued)

Figure 5.5. Continued

In the space provided, the student must justify why he or she selected this particular assignment for his or her portfolio.

As a highly motivated student who wants to eventually teach, I found that I exceeded the project's objective and that my letter of inquiry represented some of my most thoughtful writing. The overall quality and content of my letter was very good. I am proud of the initiative I used in asking for more information than was required to fulfill the project's objective. I really liked this project because I was able to learn more about myself. I was permitted to dream and write about my future career. I also wanted to learn about the college's requirements for becoming a bilingual teacher. This will help me decide what courses I must satisfactorily complete to achieve my dream and be accepted by a university. My parents worry about how they will pay for my college education. The information the university sent will help me apply for college loans.

■ CREATING A CONTINUOUS ASSESSMENT PLAN TO ENSURE STUDENT ACHIEVEMENT

Evaluating culturally and economically diverse students requires a plan for continuous assessment to (a) determine what concepts will be required to achieve mastery of a subject; (b) identify the areas of strengths and weaknesses of a subject; and (c) identify specific learning and teaching strategies that appear to have the greatest impact on a student's academic subject mastery. Figure 5.6 provides a worksheet for a school's principal and teacher leaders to use in creating a continuous and comprehensive plan for assessing students' overall academic achievement. The figure also provides an opportunity for a school's teacher leaders and the principal to determine which instruments may best meet the unique learning needs of specific student groups.

Figure 5.6. Student Achievement Assessment Plan

In the worksheet below, list the assessment instrument you and your
leadership team intend to use for specific cultural, linguistic, and economic
groups to authentically measure gains in academic achievement. Determine
how frequently you will administrator each instrument and the process you
intend to use for adequately evaluating specific groups of students.

Instrument Type	Population to Be Served	Assessment Frequency	Process Plan for Assessment Instrument

6

Summary of Culturally Proficient Urban School Practices

Although the adequate use of resources is critical for meeting the needs of diverse student learners, the teachers' instructional interventions may have a greater impact on a student's access to a higher educational career goal and satisfactory entry into the community's labor market (Gordon, 1999). When a school's principal and teacher leaders create a learning environment for each student that is supportive, the student can have the opportunities required for successful academic achievement and career development. Too frequently students have career passions that wane because the school's leadership team has not provided adequate life skills training and academic guidance essential for sufficient career preparation.

When considering the needs of culturally, linguistically, and economically challenged students, access to support services becomes limited because diverse student groups require significantly more support in remedial services for basic skill attainment. Multistressed schools must also rely more heavily on their community to leverage resources for student success. Culturally proficient school practices should include (a) reducing prejudice and discrimination through social justice, (b) considering divergent perceptions of effective social justice practices, and (c) considering the impact of social justice to a community's resources.

■ CONSIDERING HOW PRINCIPALS AND TEACHER LEADERS RESPOND TO DIVERSE STUDENTS' NEEDS

Principals and teacher leaders can best respond to diverse student's needs by accomplishing the following:

1. Having a common goal for all student groups.

2. Providing diverse groups of students with accurate information about different ethnic, racial, nationality, and immigrant populations' contributions to a community.

3. Preventing ethnic, nationality, language, or racial group formations within the school or the classroom that may impede academic progress.

4. Encouraging intergroup contact of various student groups through vicarious learning, cooperative learning, project-based learning, and service learning experiences to reduce prejudice and discrimination.

5. Encouraging diverse groups of students to work closely together in their project-based learning and service learning experiences.

6. Helping students recognize that prejudice, stereotyping, and discrimination violate the democratic values of equal opportunity and fair treatment.

7. Adjusting the curriculum to meet the diverse learning needs of various groups of students.

8. Defining academic outcomes and evaluation instruments for diverse student groups that are equitable, achievable, accountable, and continuous.

9. Creating a case management approach to student evaluation that continuously tracks students' academic strengths and weaknesses to limit the need for remedial support and to increase overall academic success.

10. Providing relevant career preparation support and college eligibility information to students and their families to ensure adequate academic planning and access to institutes of higher education.

■ DEFINING HOW CULTURALLY PROFICIENT AND COMMUNITY SUPPORTED SCHOOLS ENHANCE STUDENTS' ACADEMIC AND CAREER DEVELOPMENT

The concept of serving the greater good for the majority can empower culturally proficient students to achieve to their fullest potential and gain entry into four-year colleges for adequate career preparation. Culturally proficient and community supported schools can enhance students' academic achievement and career development through the following strategies:

1. The principal and teacher leaders can provide institutional support of various community groups to leverage added educational and community resources, support, and opportunities.

2. The school's principal and teacher leaders must encourage student groups to use their strengths as a group to collaborate and cooperate in their career development and access into institutes of higher education.

3. Students must be encouraged to mentor each other and to participate in mentoring opportunities with business partners.

4. The school's principal and teacher leaders must promote bilingualism, biculturalism, and binationalism through extensive volunteer development programs at the school site, cultural fairs and activities, and partnerships with culturally sensitive community-based organizations and businesses.

5. The school's principal and leadership team must form partnerships with institutes of higher education to cosponsor school site career fairs, precollege academic socialization boot camps, high school and college coenrollment programs, and fast-track academic preparation programs.

6. The school's principal and teacher leaders must partner with businesses to create workforce preparation programs through workplace paid apprenticeships, volunteer internships, and job shadowing programs.

7. The school's principal and teacher leaders must partner with the community and health and human care agencies to provide site-based health and human care programs that will adequately support healthy students, supportive home environments, and provide an orientation of the American school system that can ensure students' academic success.

8. The school community must celebrate its many partnerships and accomplishments for student success.

9. The school community must affirm its cultural differences and provide institutional support of the democratic process in educational program planning and school reform efforts.

10. The school community must share its resources to foster cooperation among all stakeholders that can contribute to its community's educational and economic sustainability.

A community-empowered school is one in which all stakeholders contribute to a school's goal of improving student performance (Burke & Picus, 2001). Community-empowered schools that serve diverse student groups can improve student achievement by recognizing and appreciating the diversity of their student communities. By merging these efforts with their neighborhoods' resources, culturally diverse community-empowered schools can leverage and distribute significant resources to students and their families that will ensure ongoing academic and career preparation success. The structure of culturally diverse community-empowered schools can include innovative configurations. These innovations can contribute to a school community's growth and economic sustainability (Burke & Picus, 2001).

References

Anderson, K. (1981). *Cutting deals with unlikely allies: An unorthodox approach to playing the political game.* Berkeley, CA: Anderson Negotiations/Communications Press.

Ballen, J., Casey, J. C., & de Kanter, A. (1998). *The corporate imperative: Results and benefits of business involvement in education.* Washington, DC: U.S. Department of Education.

Banks, J. A. (1997). *Educating citizens in a multicultural society.* New York: Teachers College Press.

Bennis, W., & Goldsmith, J. (1997). *Learning to lead.* Reading, MA: Addison-Wesley.

Blakely, E. J. (1997). A new role for education in economic development: Tomorrow's economy today. *Education and Urban Society, 29*(4), 509–523.

Boethel, M. (1999). Service learning: A strategy for rural school improvement and community revitalization. *Benefits, 2*(2), 1–6. Austin, TX: Southwest Educational Laboratory.

Burke, M. A. (1999). Analyzing the cost effectiveness of using parents and community volunteers to improve students' language arts test scores. *Dissertation Abstracts International, A60/06,* Z1915.

Burke, M. A. (2002). *Simplified grantwriting.* Thousand Oaks, CA: Corwin Press.

Burke, M. A., & Liljenstolpe, C. (1992). *Recruiting volunteers: A guide for nonprofits.* Menlo Park, CA: Crisp Publications.

Burke, M. A., & Liljenstolpe, C. (1993). *Creative fund-raising: A guide for success.* Menlo Park, CA: Crisp Publications.

Burke, M. A., & Picus, L. O. (2001). *Developing community-empowered schools.* Thousand Oaks, CA: Corwin Press.

Burtless, G. (1996). Introduction and Summary. In G. Burtless (Ed.), *Does Money Matter? The effect of school resources on student achievement and adult success* (pp. 1–42). Washington, DC: Brookings Institution.

California Department of Education. (1992). *Alternative approaches to assessment and evaluation in family English literacy programs.* Sacramento: California Department of Education.

Comer, J. P., Ben-Avie, M., Haynes, N. M., & Joyner, E. T. (1999). *Child by child: The Comer process for change in education.* New York: Teachers College Press

Edelman, M. W. (1999). *Lanterns.* Boston: Beacon Press.

Fitzgerald, J. (1997). Linking school-to-work programs to community economic development in urban schools. *Urban Education, 32*(4), 489–511.

Freire, P. (1985). *The politics of education: Culture, power, and education.* South Hadley, MA: Bergin and Garvey.

Fullan, M. (1993). *Changing forces: Probing the depths of educational reform.* London: Flamer Press.

Gordon, E. W. (1999). *Education and justice: A view from the back of the bus.* New York: Teachers College Press.

Hanuschek, E. A. (1994). *Making schools work: Improving performance and controlling costs.* Washington, DC: Brookings Institution.

Hutson, H. M., Jr. (1981). Inservice best practices: The learnings of general education. *Journal of Research and Development in Education, 14,* 1–9.

Jennings, J. F. (Ed.). (1995). *National issues in education: Goals 2000 and school-to-work.* Bloomingdale, IN: Phi Delta Kappa & Washington, DC: Institute for Educational Leadership.

Joyce, B., & Showers, B. (1980). Improving inservice training: The messages of research. *Educational Leadership, 37,* 379–385.

Karasoff, P. (1999). Opening the door to collaborative practice. *Teacher Education Quarterly, 26*(4), 53–67.

Kerchner, C. T. (1997). Education as a city's big industry. *Education and Urban Society, 29*(4), 424–441.

Ladd, H. F. (1996). Introduction. In H. F. Ladd (Ed.), *Holding schools accountable: Performance-based reform in education* (pp. 1–19). Washington, DC: Brookings Institution.

Lindsey, R. B., Robins, K. R., & Terrell, R. D. (1999). *Cultural proficiency: A manual for school leaders.* Thousand Oaks, CA: Corwin Press.

MacKinnon, B. (2001). *Ethics: Theory and contemporary issues.* Belmont, CA: Wadsworth/Thomson Learning.

McLemore, S. D., & Romo, H. D. (1998). *Racial and Ethnic Relations in America* (5th ed). Boston: Allyn and Bacon.

National Commission on Excellence and Equity in Education. (1983). *A nation at risk: The imperative of educational reform.* Washington, DC: U.S. Department of Education.

Oakes, J., Quartz, K. H., Ryan, S., & Lipton, M. (2000). *Becoming good American schools: The struggle for civic virtue in education reform.* San Francisco, CA: Jossey-Bass.

Olsen, L., Chang, H., De La Rosa Salazar, D., Leong, C., McCall Perez, Z., McClain, G., & Raffel, L. (1994). *The unfinished journey: Restructuring schools in a diverse society.* San Francisco: California Tomorrow.

Orfield, G., Eaton, S., & the Harvard Project on School Desegregation. (1996). *Dismantling desegregation: The quiet reversal of Brown v. Board of Education.* New York: New Press.

Reeves, D. B. (2000). *Accountability action: A blueprint for learning organizations.* Denver, CO: Advanced Learning Centers.

Sanders, E. T. W. (1999). *Urban school leadership: Issues and strategies.* Larchmont, NY: Eye on Education.

Schmitt, D. M., & Tracy, J. C. (1996). *Gaining support for your school: Strategies for community involvement.* Thousand Oaks, CA: Corwin Press.

Short, P. J., & Greer, J. T. (1997). *Leadership in empowered schools.* Upper Saddle River, NJ: Prentice Hall.

Spring, J. (1998). *Education and the rise of the global economy.* Mahwah, NJ: Lawrence Erlbaum.

Stanton-Salazar, R. D. (2001). *Manufacturing hope and despair: The school and kin support networks of U.S.-Mexican youth.* New York: Teachers College Press.

Sweeney, J., Schenirer, J., & Lefkovitz, B. (2001). Developing results-based school/community partnerships. *Journal for the Community Approach, 2*(1), 4–8.

U.S. Department of Education. (1994). *Strong families, strong schools: Building community partnerships for learning.* Washington, DC: U.S. Department of Education.

Valenzuela, A. (1999). *Subtractive schooling: U.S.-Mexican youth and the politics of caring.* Albany: State University of New York Press.

WestEd. (1996). *School reform: A new outlook.* San Francisco: Author.

Wolf, S. (1983). Ethics, legal ethics, and the ethics of law. In D. Luban (Ed.), *The good lawyer* (pp. 41–49). Lanham, MD: Rowan & Littlefield.

Index